# The Calder Family and Other Critters

# The Calder Family and Other Critters

## Portraits and Reflections

Sandra Calder Davidson

Introduction by

Jed Pearl

ARCADE PUBLISHING • NEW YORK

First Edition

Arcade Publishing books may be purchased in bulk at special discounts for sales promotion, corporate gifts, fund-raising, or educational purposes. Special editions can also be created to specifications. For details, contact the Special Sales Department, Arcade Publishing, 307 West 36th Street, 11th Floor, New York, NY 10018 or arcade@skyhorsepublishing.com.

Arcade Publishing® is a registered trademark of Skyhorse Publishing, Inc.®, a Delaware corporation.

Visit our website at www.arcadepub.com.

10 9 8 7 6 5 4 3 2 1

Library of Congress Cataloging-in-Publication Data is available on file.
ISBN: 978-1-61145-897-8

Printed in China

Editor: Cal Barksdale
Designer: Brian Peterson

*In thinking of my family . . .*

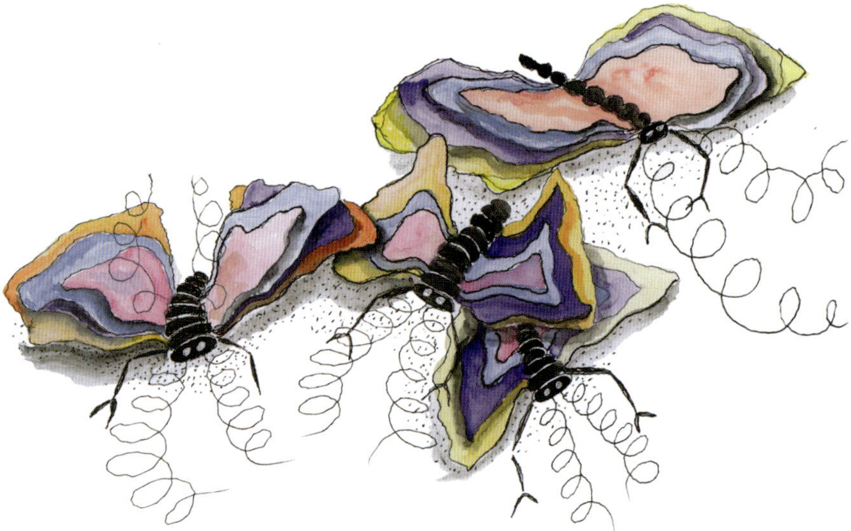

# Contents

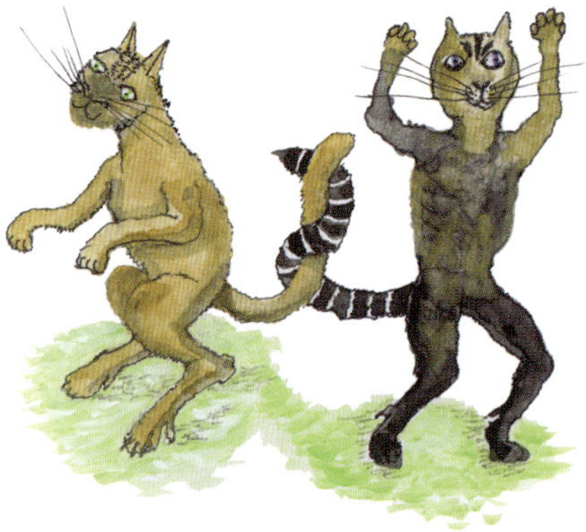

# Sandra's Critters

## An Introduction by Jed Perl

Sandra Calder Davidson's drawings of family and friends, reimagined as figures from the animal kingdom, are an enchanted parallel universe. What will initially draw many people to these ebullient studies is Sandra's intimate and affectionate view of the life and times of her father, Alexander Calder, the inventor of the mobile and one of the great creative spirits of the twentieth century. But what gives her cloisonné colored portraits their enduring fascination is the playful rococo power and elegant rapier wit of the artist's graphic eye. Sandra is very much an original, entirely in control of this gathering of family and friends, assessing with unabashed ardor the joys and perplexities of those who have meant the most to her.

Over the past few years, while I have been working on a biography of Sandra's father, Sandra and I have become friends. I can see that her analogies between men and women and the rest of the inhabitants of the animal kingdom arise naturally, even spontaneously. This is quite simply one of the ways she has of understanding the world. Sandra reminds us—at least she reminds me—that the magic of metamorphosis is in our blood, the stuff of dreams and fantasies. She clearly enjoys figuring out where each relative, friend, or acquaintance fits into her ever-expanding menagerie. And she does not exclude herself, for she is the camel—apparently it was her father who first made *that* comparison!—and as much a figure of loving comedy as anybody else.

Of course, like any animal kingdom, Sandra's has its royalty. And there can never have been any question as to who would wear the crown in this particular furred and feathered realm. Calder is quite naturally the lion, the king of the beasts. In one beautiful drawing he is the most adorably appealing sleepy lion, sitting in his chair taking a regal catnap. Calder is wearing one of the bold red shirts to which he was especially partial. And around him Sandra has arranged the delightfully informal sort of interior in which Sandra's father and her mother, Louisa, always felt at home. There are wine bottles to the right, an early wire portrait of Louisa hangs on the wall, and Calder's chair (and his tail!) rest on one of the rugs that Louisa hooked from her husband's designs; Louisa's basket full of wool can be seen in the background. This is a world Sandra brings vividly alive, down to the African carving and tambourine and maracas (the Calders loved South American dance music) hanging on the wall. Sandra's lusty embrace of a rainbow's worth of hues is surely a response to her father's own enthusiastic feeling for color, especially the expanses of full-strength red he adored.

Born in 1935, Sandra started life at a time when her father was already becoming an avant-garde hero but was hardly a household name. It was only as she was entering adulthood that Calder became one of the world's most widely admired, exhibited, and talked-about artists. The family of four—Mary,

Sandra's sister, was born in 1939—was always offbeat and bohemian. Calder's parents were both artists; Alexander Stirling Calder was a distinguished sculptor specializing in large public commissions, and Nanette Calder was a painter of considerable subtlety and sophistication. Sandra's mother, born Louisa Cushing James, was a great-niece of Henry James and grew up in a Boston Brahmin family of progressive views; Louisa's father was so enthusiastic about the promise of the League of Nations that he spent time in Geneva, following the proceedings. Sandra's graphic interpretations of the members of her family reflect a closeness that runs deep in the Calder clan, down to the generation of Sandra's children and grandchildren and nephews and their children. One of the most remarkable stories Sandra has told me about her father dates from when Calder, Louisa, Sandra, and Sandra's husband, Jean, and their children were all living in Saché, a village a couple of hours southwest of Paris. One day Sandra came back to her house to find her father holding a package and weeping with joy. The package contained the first copies of the first children's book of Sandra's that was published. Such was Calder's pleasure that another generation was taking up the artist's trade.

It is certainly no secret that Sandra's father took a considerable interest in animals. Calder was just short of twenty-eight when he published a little book called *Animal Sketching,* with spirited ink drawings of all manner of beasts and birds and a text suggesting how to capture their rapid-fire movements. Many of Calder's early sculptures, both in wire and wood, are of animals, and even after his work had turned predominantly abstract, he would from time to time make a fish out of broken bits of colored glass or a bird with pieces of brilliantly printed tin cans. Calder published *A Bestiary*, with his drawings illustrating poems and prose selected by Richard Wilbur, and late in life he produced a series of figures, fantastical humanoids that he called *Critters*, a word Sandra may be echoing in the title of her book. If Sandra has to some degree inherited her taste for animals from her father, it is also worth pointing out that animals were a subject for earlier artists in the Calder clan. The first of the Calder sculptors, Calder's grandfather, Alexander Milne Calder, had studied in his native Scotland and eventually settled in Philadelphia, where he worked for decades on sculptures for the Philadelphia City Hall, including some striking portraits of animals, especially a series of howling felines. As for Calder's father, among his most intimate works is a clay study of a lithe, youthful Walt Whitman with a cat playing at his feet.

Sandra's feeling for animals may well be in her DNA, inherited from the sculptors in the Calder family who admired the vigor and cunning of the animal kingdom. But whereas the Calder men embodied the sculptor's taste for generalization, Sandra is always reaching for greater particularization. She is very much the storyteller, with a skill in setting the scene that recalls some of the uproarious drawings of the nineteenth-century French illustrator J. J. Grandeville, whose renderings of men and women as animals and birds and flowers were particular favorites of the Surrealists, with whom Sandra's father shared interests and enthusiasms. Sandra, who is anything but a Surrealist, likes to keep her fantasies firmly grounded in our everyday world. Her drawings bristle with wonderfully, closely observed facts. Louisa, who is represented as the sly fox with an overflowing glass of scotch and water in one hand, wears four pieces of silver jewelry designed by her husband—two bracelets, a pin, and a ring—each one limned by Sandra with unerring exactitude. Do not miss the spiffy, low-slung green sports car on which four cats cavort in the portrait of Sandra's husband, Jean, who was an avid amateur race-car driver and is represented as a very cool bird. In Sandra's salute to her sister, Mary, who is seen prancing around in her kitchen, no detail is missing from the wonderful old Philco gas stove. And Sandra's granddaughter, Anya, is decked out in hipster clothes that are realized with adoring attention to each cacophonous shift in color and pattern.

Sandra brings flashes of sharp, sly critique to her portraits of family and friends, but what she ultimately adds to the long history of the caricaturist's art is a spirit of generosity—a heartfelt tenderness. I think that what Sandra is telling us is that if you care and you love, you will also find yourself laughing. *The Calder Family and Other Critters* is a celebration, a love fest, a glorious gathering of the clan.

# The Calder Family and Other Critters

# A Word to Begin

Gerald Durrell wrote *My Family and Other Animals* about growing up in his eccentric family–which included his brother, Lawrence, later to become a famous novelist–on the island of Corfu, a department of Greece. This is about my family and the animals they sometimes are. I wonder if Durrell, a naturalist, truly saw the animal in his family members. When we go to the mirror, it is to make sure that we hide the animal as much as we can. Lipstick, rouge, powder, mascara–what animal wears all that? But the animal instinct still appears in more or less heavy doses. It's normal. . . . After all, we do descend from the apes, and a doctor told me the other day that we descend from the fishes. I can't help you figure that one out.

I am not a scientist, just someone with a little bit of animal instinct. I'd say that the animal is revealed in us in a very subtle mixture of looks and behavior. People often ask, as though I'm an expert on the subject, "So what am I?" I would have to know you quite well before I can advance any opinion. So here are my critters, and don't feel neglected if you don't find yourself in this book . . .you might be in the next!

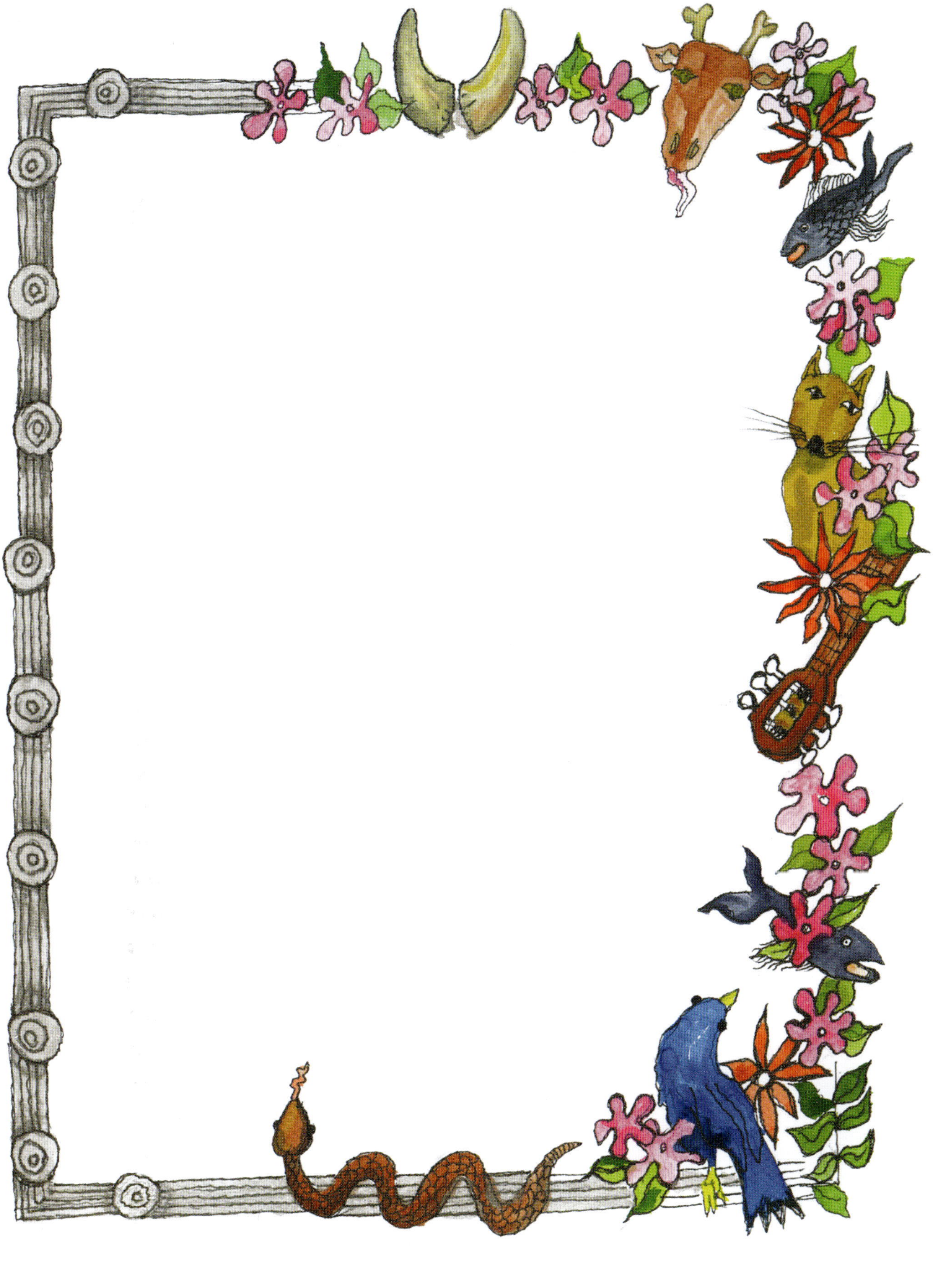

# Pop

My father, Alexander Calder, was born to a mother whose family was German-Jewish and a father whose family was Scottish. He came two years after his sister, Margaret, better known as Peggy.

Their mother was an excellent painter, and their father a classical sculptor using stone and clay. Peggy was born in Paris, and my father was born in Philadelphia. I think they were a close-knit family. My father said that once, when they were small and not behaving, his mother put on her coat and left the apartment. My father was deeply affected by that even years later. He most likely tried to make sure that would never happen again. He no doubt felt as though he had lost his BALANCE. The word "balance" had a profound meaning in this boy's mind.

I am sure that he was a good boy. That he listened to his parents. From the moment he could use his hands, he was making things. At the age of nine he was using wire and pliers. He made dolls for his sister, Peggy. Even doll clothes. Beds for the dolls. Wagons, chariots, animals. I imagine he was rarely bored. It's really terrible to see nowadays how children are so bored unless they have a device to entertain them. They don't know how to use their hands. How important it is to see the multitude of things one can make or do. Their imagination is just not exercised any more.

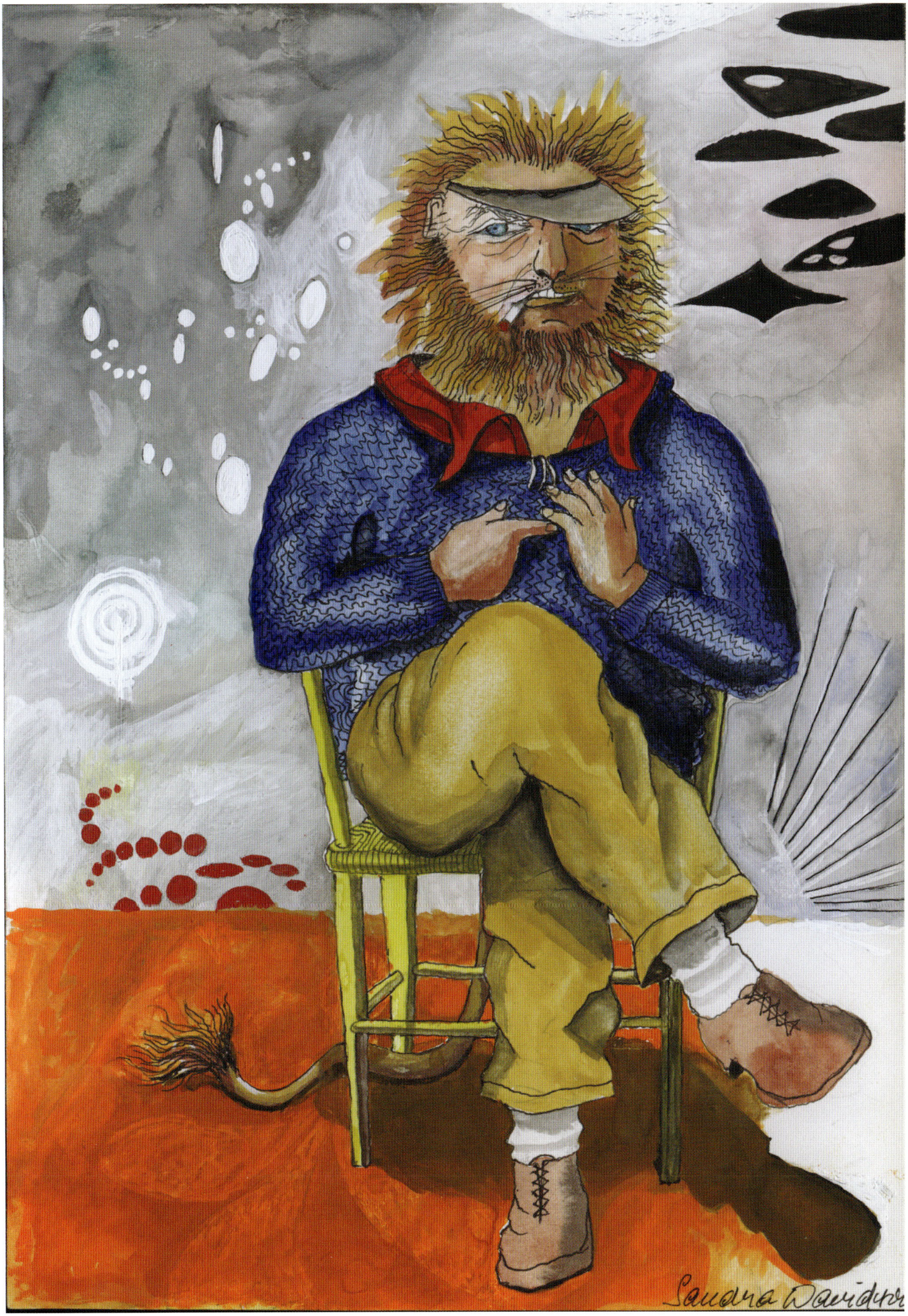

# Pop

Alexander was nicknamed Sandy. His family moved often. His father, Stirling, had tuberculosis. That was the reason for their moving to Arizona and then Pasadena when Sandy was a boy. Wherever they went, my father's workbench and tools went too. He could pick up right away where he left off; that gives the child the good feeling of continuity. His mother made his clothes. The arm holes of his shirts were slits, not necessarily alike. A cord closed the shirt at the neck. His unusual attire didn't seem to bother him in the least. Instead, he seemed to be surprised, later on in life, when his daughters wanted only run-of-the-mill store-bought clothes. He worked well in school. There didn't appear to be too many problems there either.

Years later, after he graduated from Stevens Institute of Technology with straight A's and a degree in engineering, came the problem of earning a living. Early on, the earnings were small and the jobs often ended abruptly. When he was designing toys, my father complained to the boss about not having enough light, that he was hurting his eyes because of it. The boss said, "To hell with your eyes!" and my father answered, "To hell with your toys!" and left. As a young artist, it certainly was not easy to make a living with your own inventions that no one understood. But thank God for that too: Thanks to the fact that no one understood it, there is a beautiful piece now sitting on my desk. Three wooden shapes, one ebony, are hitched up to a wooden plank by way of wire that goes through the plank to three separate pulleys on the other side. By way of a string attached to a crank at the foot of the plank, the three shapes turn, should you turn the crank. Silent, no motor, a mysterious object that can take you far!

I'm quite sure that Sandy rarely took a job because he wanted to. He took a job because he needed the money. But even with needing the income, the job had to be acceptable. Luckily, after he married and began a family, my mother had a small monthly allowance that kept them going if need be. Neither of them bought frivolous, unnecessary things. It was all down-to-earth. One day, during the Second World War, when olive oil was scarce, my father brought back a five gallon can of oil from Waterbury. My mother sent him back with it, because it was not essential.

People say to me now, "It must have been difficult being the child of such a famous man," as though being "famous" was a wish you could make: You snap your fingers and there is "famous," alive and well. It took years for him to achieve what he wanted—that is, being recognized as a serious sculptor, not a jack-of-all-trades. I was married with two children when he had his first clamorous success, in Brazil.

There is nothing more annoying than him being called, and by critics, a "tinkerer." If there was one thing he wasn't, it was that! He was not a tinkerer; he took his work with the utmost seriousness. One could stand around and watch, but he never took his mind off what he was doing. Occasionally, he would ask my mother to take a look at something, to get her opinion. He never stopped unless a friend came by to say hello. I worked upon occasion in his studio, for example making an ant cage with nails and string and a tiny board. The ants probably thought it most the most amazing jungle gym. My father was no doubt delighted to see his daughter working with hammer and nails.

This is not an autobiography. It's a "glimpse." For more detailed information, there are a lot of sources out there. I am rather embarrassed to say that I have read none. I have only read bits and pieces. I know what went on: I was there. My father was very happy when he at last became "known," recognized. But I truly do not think that the idea of being famous was his motivation. He HAD to do what he did. It could not have been otherwise. My mother certainly gave him a lot of encouragement and support, and was apparently outraged when he was shortchanged by the galleries. That practice happened even in those days, to a lesser degree maybe, but the prices were lower too.

The piece about my mother will help you understand how one and one made a team. There were certainly ups and downs. They were very discreet about themselves. Later on, when times were easier, they spent money on traveling back and forth between New York and Saché, France. My father had a big house built on the hilltop in Saché. When they were in residence, it was lively and colorful. I returned there not long ago and was overwhelmed by the space and the size of the empty living room—not very cozy. It was my mother who decided what rug to put on the floor, and where; what pots should be placed on the counter; which blanket covered the couch. My father placed the paintings on the walls and decided where the mobiles would be hung from the beams for lack of a ceiling—the lack of ceilings was part of the size problem. My mother's greenhouse was not the private little area where one plants seeds and starts cuttings. It was so big a gardener was needed to plant lemon trees, olive trees, and other vegetation.

Sometimes my father saw too big—at Saché in particular. My mother never felt at home there. It was also too open to the public, who couldn't refrain from prowling around and peeking through windows. My father worked in the studio down by the mill, so my mother was alone in the house, up on the hill.

My father never stopped giving. He took pride in giving. He never saw the difference between people of color and whites, or between a farmer and a CEO. He treated everyone with equal respect, whether it was a kid or his parents, a minor or a major, a dancer or a dentist, a drummer or a street vendor, and whether they be croc or camel, or mouse or squirrel, or bluebird or sparrow. Thin or fat, slow or rapid, twisted or straight, they were separate but equal. And that is the truth!

# Louisa

When my mother and father first met, he nicknamed her "Medusa." She had an abundance of luxurious hair, and she was beautiful. She was certainly one of a kind! Her father, Holton James of Concord, Massachusetts, found that the guys at home were not to his liking and took his daughter Louisa to Europe when she was of the age to marry. There, they would lounge in hotel lobbies, hoping to meet a young European man who would be intelligent and interesting. It didn't happen! When the time came to go home, they boarded the *De Grasse* to cross the ocean in the opposite direction. It was on the deck of the *De Grasse* that my mother met a young American man, a sculptor who worked with wire. His name was Alexander Calder, but he was better known to everyone as Sandy. He was definitely someone of interest to my mother. Though I do wonder what my grandfather thought!

Louisa James, the scion of two prominent Boston families—her mother was Louisa Cushing, from a Brahmin family of many members, and on her father's side she was a grandniece of Henry and William James—probably wanted to party that last night on board. Who knew? . . . They might never meet again. The young artist, however, was anxious to arrive back home rested and fresh. This society girl, upset that her new acquaintance wouldn't succumb to her desires, threw a spoon at him, making a gash in his forehead.

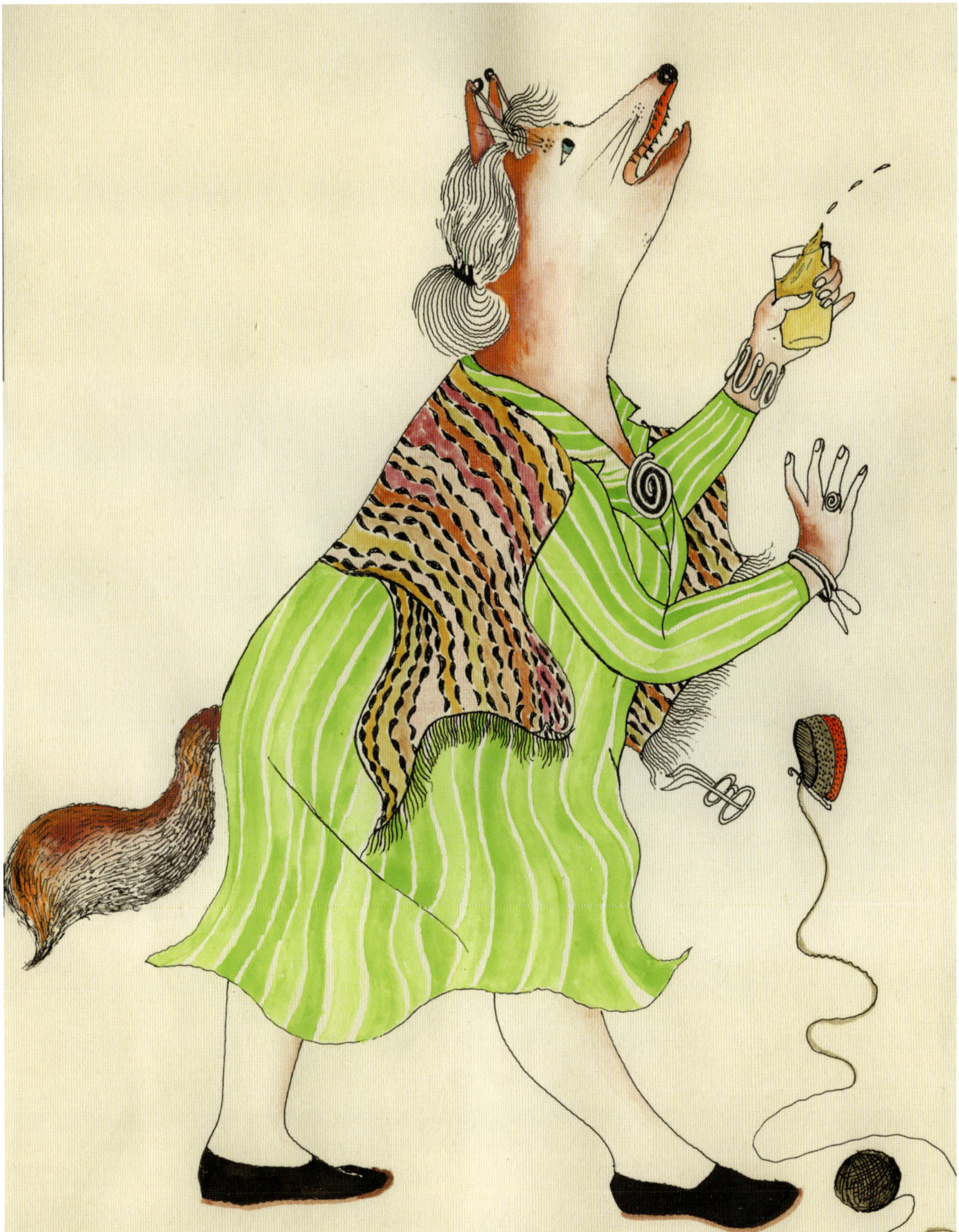

The young man who had wanted to meet his mother on the dock fresh and rested now had a wound he would have to explain. No matter, their love affair flourished, until they were married in 1931.

Together, they traveled and danced and partied. She loved life. She loved to garden and cook, hook rugs, and play the accordion. When Sandy gave a performance of his circus, she was the disc jockey. The audience consisted of friends for the most part. They sat on planks set up in his studio (after pushing everything aside), drank beer, and ate peanuts. The audience was always very enthusiastic. Sometimes they were asked by my father to roar like a lion, blow whistles, or beat the drums. It was a happening or a performance piece like no one had ever seen before in his life. The disc jockey had a great deal to do with the success of the show, for she was the only one to know the order of performance. She had chosen the pieces of music from their discs—waltzes, sambas, jazz, or French bal-musette.

Louisa could be sharp and nippy too. (Don't forget the spoon.) She could put my father in his place if need be. She hosted all of my father's collectors, which must have been quite a drag. As I mentioned, he would upon occasion ask her to look at a piece. He wanted her opinion.

In 1955—it must have been when I came back from France—I explained to my mother that I wanted to marry our family friend, Jean Davidson, the journalist and writer who also raced cars. She said to me, looking at my coral necklace that Jean had given me, "I see the collar, where's the leash?" No such thing as, "Oh! My darling, I am so happy for you!" No, No, No! And it wasn't because she didn't like him. It was probably because he was twenty years older than I was. Yet, my parents were so ahead of their times, why wouldn't they be the same with this singular event?

When my mother was young, Holton James traveled the world, meeting and encouraging dissidents. He had become very involved in the Sacco and Vanzetti case and found himself in confrontations with the law a number of times. He went to jail because of it. His wife, Louisa Cushing James, organized a settlement in Boston for people without food or shelter.

So it was with my mother. She marched as often as she could against the war in Vietnam and signed as many petitions against the war as she was able. According to the *New York Times*, she refused to attend a White House ceremony honoring Sandy shortly after his death in 1977, and instead pressed for blanket amnesty for opponents to the war.

Some people say that they never saw Sandy without Louisa. Each one was essential to the other's life. The day my father died, my mother died too, in spirit.

# Calder Parties

We all loved to dance. We loved music and friends. So when my mother decided we were going to have a party, she invited all the usual neighboring friends—the Wolffs, the Millers, the Miltons, the Papadakis, the Whites, the Nitzschkes—and others as well, for example, the workmen who had built my grandmother's house up on the hill. My mother made pizzas, pizzas, pizzas. They were the best. She also served baked ham, green salads, applesauce. The food cluttered the table. It was all delicious, everyone agreed. Arthur Miller recalls, "And as sometimes happened around ten or twelve o'clock . . . that is, ten or twelve o'clock next morning, people were still hanging around the table expecting to have lunch even if they were full and done in."

I miss those nights, dancing the samba (my parents would go to Brazil just to dance the samba), ballroom, one-step, two-step, swing, waltz. And when the rock and roll came in, everyone danced twice as fast. Everyone was simply there to have fun, not to show off.

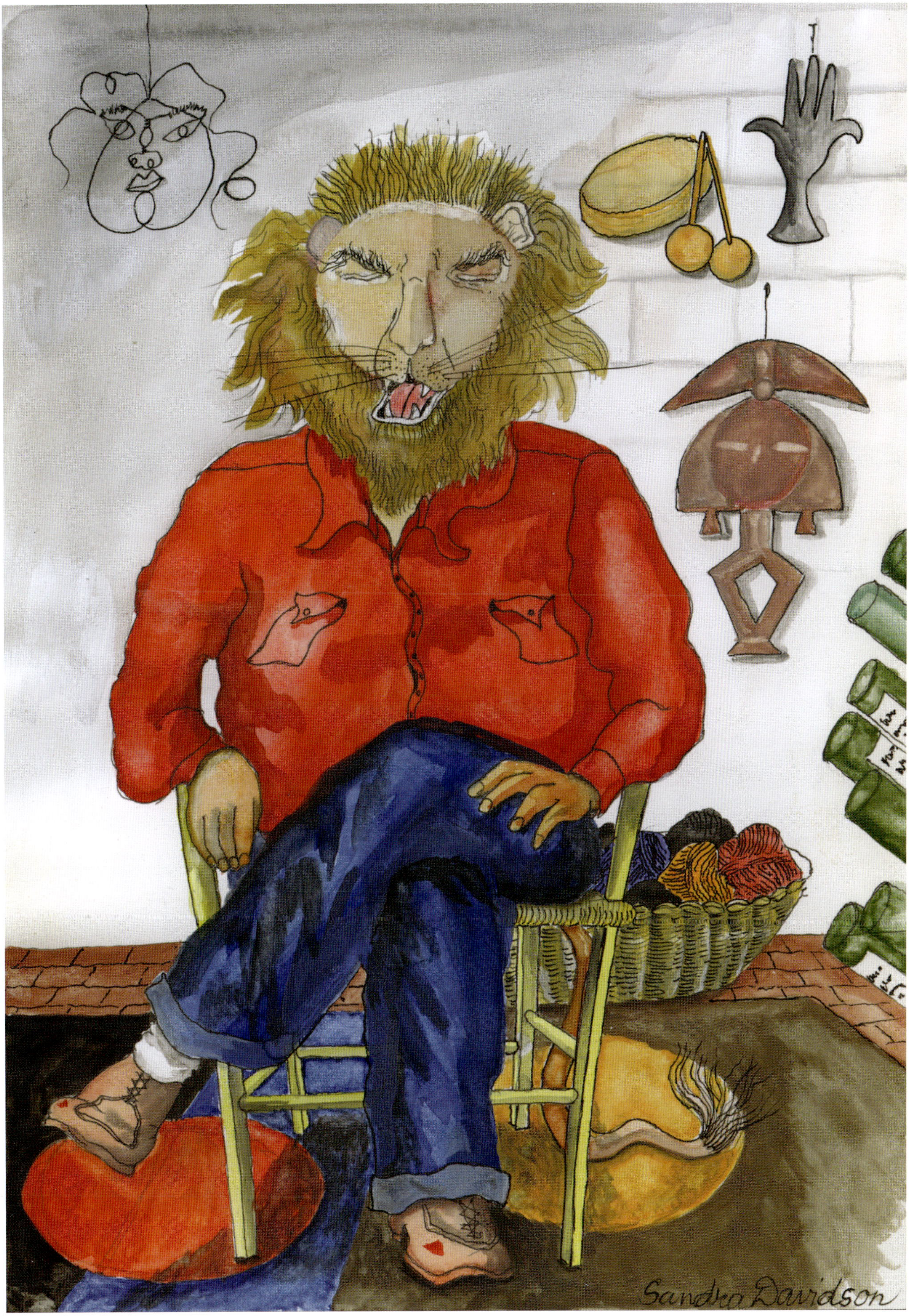
Sandra Davidson

# Two Sisters' Secret Tale

We were the only two to know this very private family story. Now, unfortunately, I am the only one . . . so I must tell it. When we lived in Roxbury, Connecticut, and my sister and I went to the village school, the four of us would have breakfast together at the kitchen table. Often, after breakfast, my father would suddenly get up and rush to the opposite side of the table, where my mother was seated. Seeing him coming and knowing exactly what was on his mind, she would quickly jump up and dash around the table to escape him, until he grabbed her and gave her a noisy, juicy kiss. My mother would wipe the saliva off her chin, while the two of us, Sandra, eight, and Mary, four, were amused by the whole operation but did not quite know what it all meant. The two of us never discussed what we had just seen and simply took it for granted . . . so it seems.

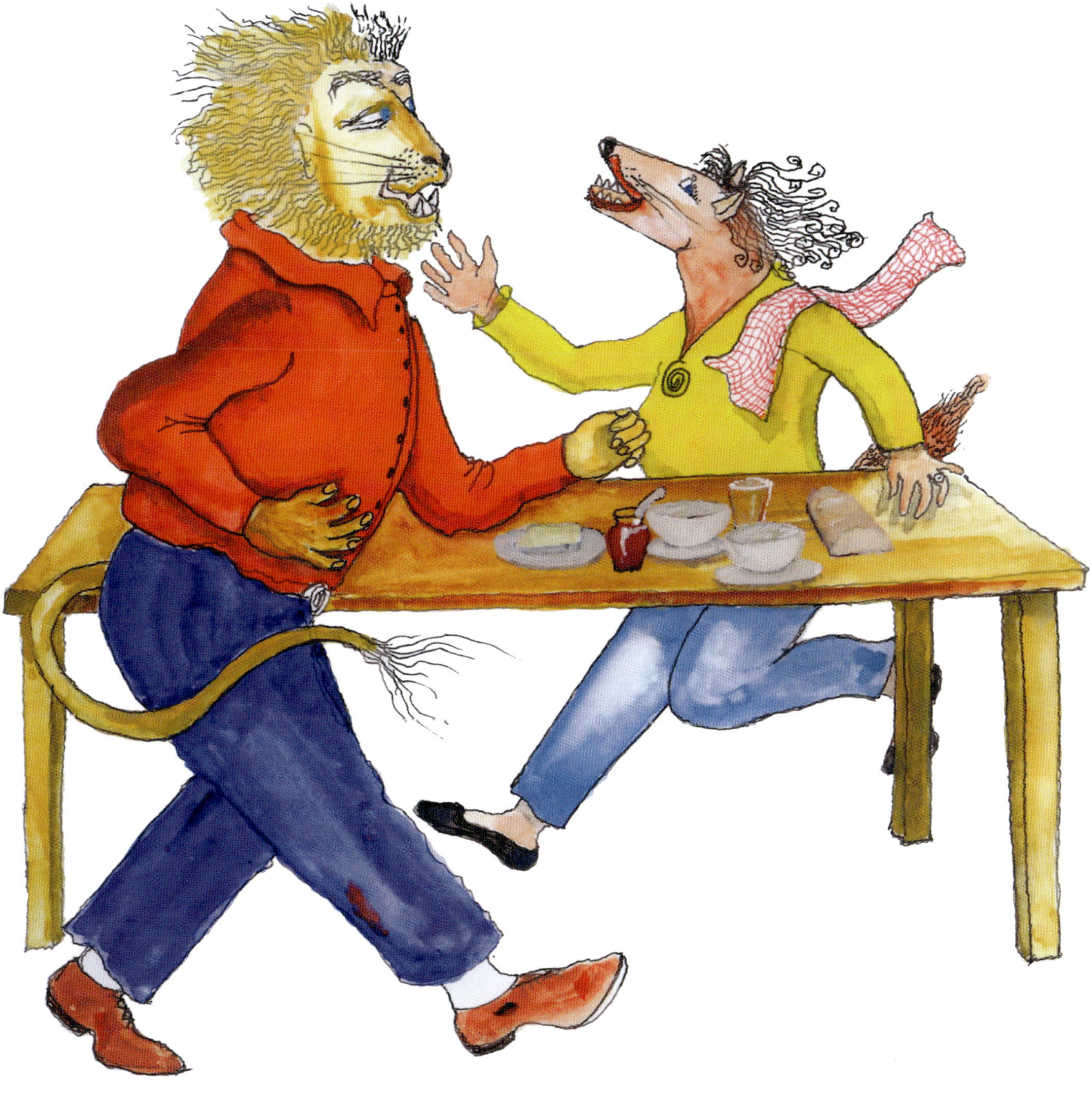

# Grandma Calder

I don't really have any one or two distinct memories of her. I can feel the atmosphere of the time from a photograph, and it is warm and cozy. I liked their apartment in Brooklyn when we sat out on what seemed to be a closed-in deck with the sun streaming in. Grandma used to take me to the theatre or a concert.

After our grandfather, Stirling, died, she came to live above us on 72nd Street, so there was a lot of going upstairs and going downstairs kind of thing. When we moved to the country, in Connecticut, our future house was a disaster area. Everything seemed beyond repair, at least to me, but at long last we moved in to the "new house," and then a new "new" house was built on the slope just behind ours for Grandma to live in. She lived there until she died.

I saw her again before she died, when I went back to Roxbury to get permission from my parents to marry Jean. He had until now been "their" friend. Grandma said to me, though she didn't know him, "He could be your father!"

Yes, I knew that, but I was in love and had been brought up in an unclassical, unconventional way, so truly it did not concern me. I was in love with Jean and with France, so nothing could change my mind. When we married, we continued to live in France. So I didn't see dear Grandma again.

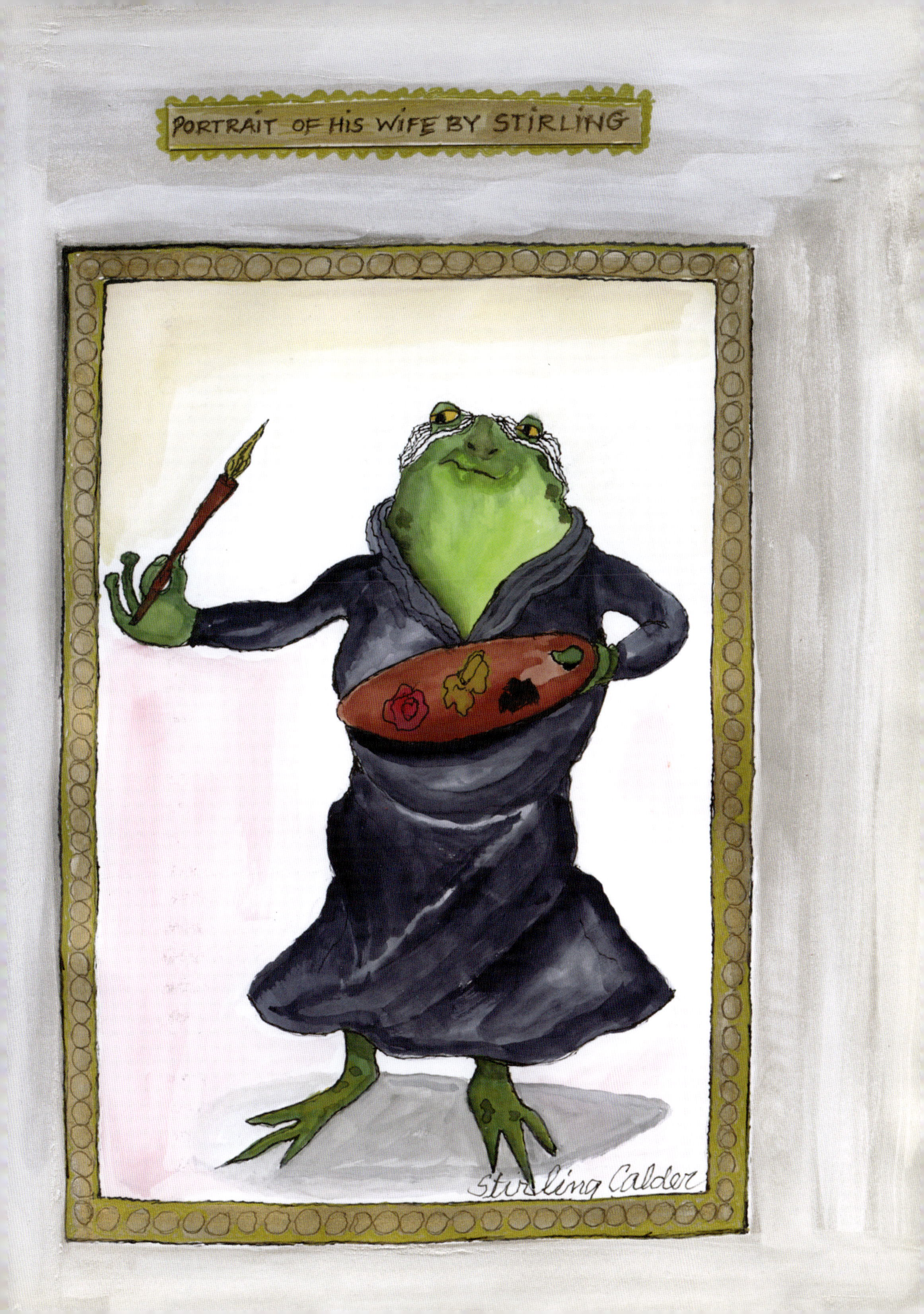
PORTRAIT OF HIS WIFE BY STIRLING
Stirling Calder

# Sandra

It was my father who compared me to a camel. He thought I looked down my nose at people, and I dare say he was right. I didn't much like the rich. I didn't appreciate their attitude. I was sure we were poor. And if you're poor, you don't like the rich. How did I know we were poor? I didn't, but for sure we did not live like others, so therefore we were, in my mind. We were different from everybody else. We did not have the couches, the television, the wallpaper, the sparkling new car. I did not really fit in anywhere socially either. I loved the life we lived. Everything in our house was handmade, and from one foreign country or another. Our kitchen was certainly not like any other kitchen I had seen. If my mother needed a serving spoon, my father would rush to his studio to make it. Not just one, but he would come back with two or three beautiful silver spoons. We needed chairs? My father would make them!

My father had crafted the beautiful kitchen cupboards. If he had to make all these things, it must have been because we didn't have the means to buy them. I can't remember any bought piece of furniture in our house, unless it had been given to us by grandparents. My mother knit most of our sweaters, giving them bright, colorful stripes. The girls in school wore pink and flowered sweaters and dresses bought at the local department store. If we were driven to school, it was in our old LaSalle.

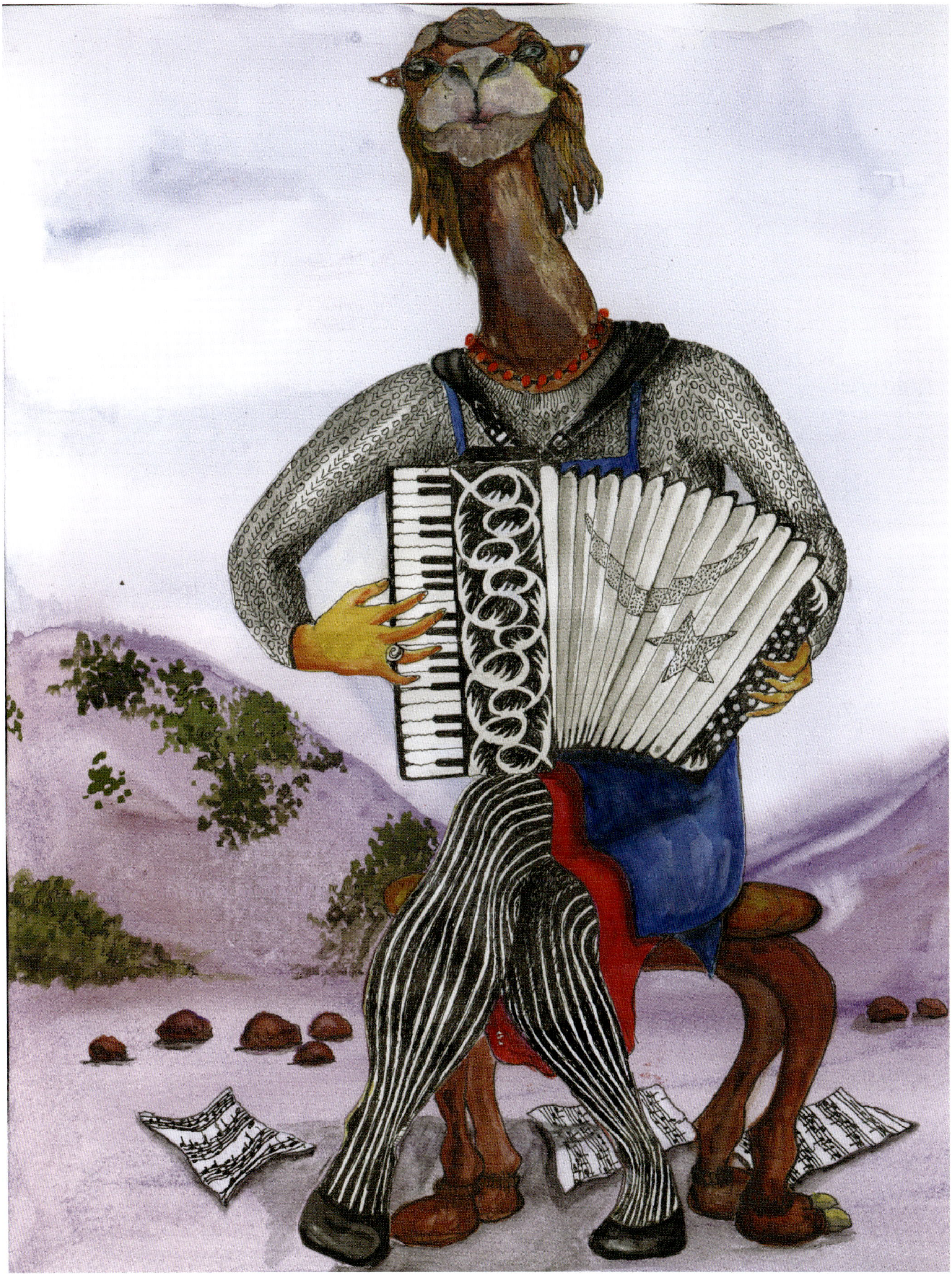

The LaSalle had been given to my father by the garage man, probably to make room for other cars in his garage. New, it had been a very fancy car, probably driven by a chauffeur—it had been a limousine, in other words. But by the time it became our LaSalle, it was an old dilapidated wreck, on which my father had to install three iron rods so that on rainy days he could throw a tarpaulin over them, to form a pretend roof. The sides were open to the wind and rain, and cars that passed us on the highway often called out, "Want an umbrella?"

When we were driven to school in the morning or picked up in the afternoon, the entire school would rush to the windows to see "Mr. Calder's car." The other children were picked up in Fords or Dodges or Chevies. When we finally got a brand-new Ford station wagon, it was the "new" car for ten years.

My mother received many pamphlets from all the organizations she helped out financially. One of them came from a group helping the poor people in Appalachia. It explained the dire circumstances in which these people lived, and there were plenty of photos too. I was fascinated by their stories. At last, I had found a people who lived the way we did. The Appalachians! Years later, a friend of ours, the Spanish architect José Luis Sert, said, talking about my father, "He was the first hippy." Now, that made me very proud. And the camel has since lowered her nose—it's too tiring to hold it up for so long, anyway.

Then I went away to boarding school, where no one had a clue as to where I came from, except for my art teacher. No one had a clue as to what a mobile was, and I didn't try to explain. After I graduated, we all went to France for a year, where I could better feel my way around. When the family left, I stayed behind. I took dance lessons and painting lessons with a private teacher. I can't say that I learned that much from the painting lessons. In neither place was I taught anything about perspective, which is, to my mind, the most important element to learn. So I stayed in France and among many other things got involved with Jean Davidson, an extraordinary man . . . and soon married him.

You might wonder where the accordion fits in. No, unfortunately, I took lessons but do not play. My mother played when I was in her womb, and having it so close to my ear I was contaminated. I love accordion music, and I love to draw the accordion.

# Jean

As Jean walked along the street in Washington, D.C., where he lived and worked as a war correspondent for the French newspapers and Canadian radio, he spotted a strange-looking apparatus sticking out of a trash can. He lifted the lid of the can and pulled out an object that fascinated him. It was made with two wooden dowels and some string; at each stick end hung a string, and at each string end hung a portrait of Hitler and Mussolini and also a dollar sign. These portraits were cut out of cardboard and painted with watercolors.

Amazed, Jean looked up and around. This garbage can undoubtedly belonged to the office of France Forever, a propaganda organization started by Charles de Gaulle to collect money to fight against the Nazis, and what he was holding meant: Give dollars to get the heads of Hitler and Mussolini. Jean walked into the office and said in an excited voice, "I'll buy this," and he plunked a fifty-dollar bill on the table. The deal was no sooner done than Paul Nelson, who was the head of France Forever and also a friend of my father's, said to Jean, "Would you like to meet the guy who made it?" That one question would change Jean's life forever. My life changed too, for we were later married.

Jean was passionate about what he did, even about racing cars. As a child, he explained to all his pals that his father was Harley Davidson, the

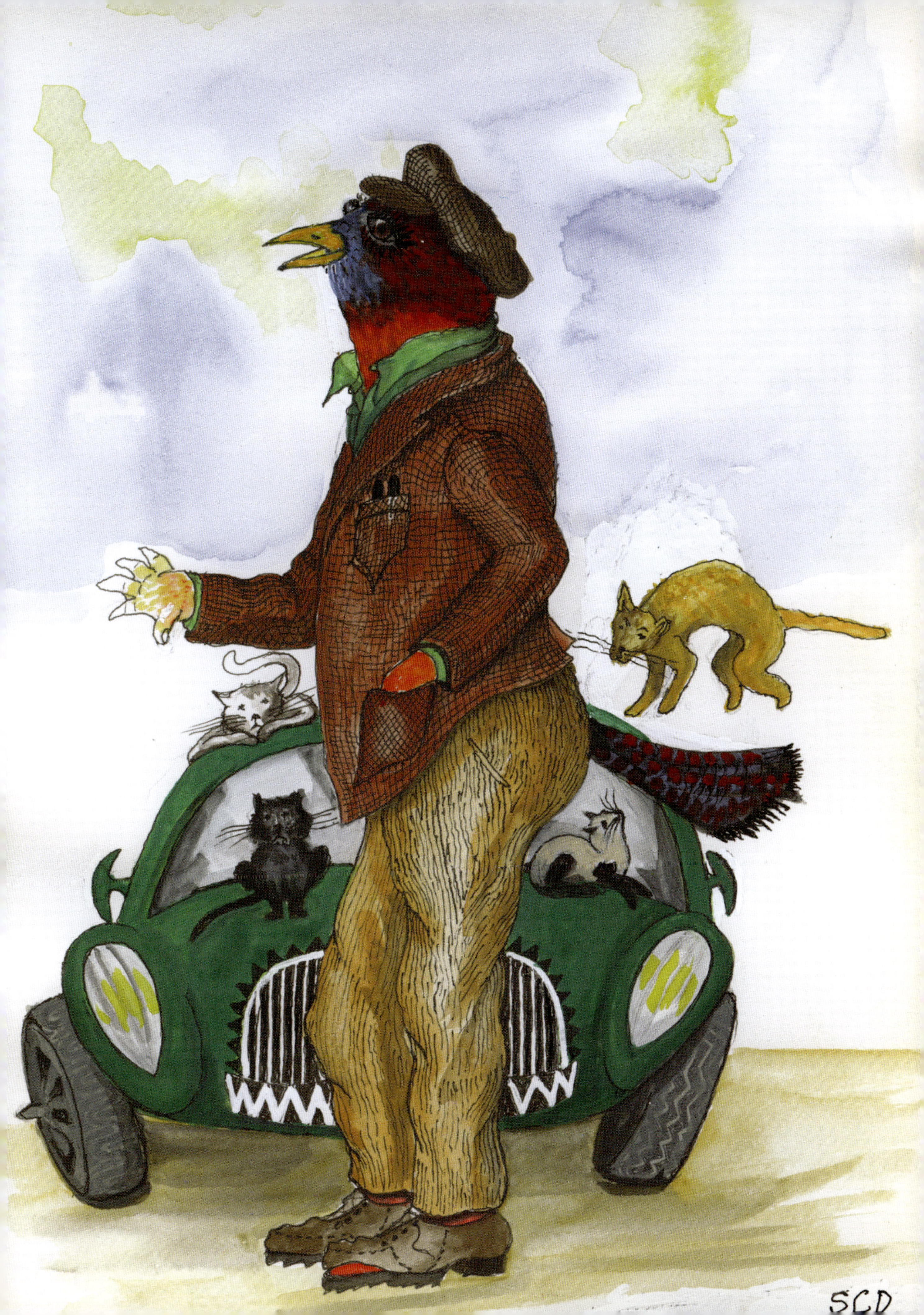
SCD

motorcycle Harley Davidson. It was much more impressive than saying that his father was a sculptor. A sculptor who did heads, the heads of Charlie Chaplin, Albert Einstein, Gandhi, Eisenhower, and many other famous people, not just anybody's head.

After meeting Calder at a dinner party given by Paul Nelson, Jean mentioned to his father that he had "just met a fantastic American sculptor." Jo, infuriated that Jean could be impressed by such a "fraud," threw a crowbar at him. Their relationship was not an easy one. Jean had a passion for speed. Maybe to him it was like meditation. You empty your head of everything and burn up the road ahead of you. No question of daydreaming. When finally at the age of eighteen he did have an accident in which he was nearly killed, his father disinherited him. He proceeded to get a job as a crime reporter in Chicago. But after a few years of hanging out with the gangsters of Chicago, with whom he often played poker, he went to Washington, D.C., where he became a journalist for the French wire service and the Canadian radio.

Jean was constantly seeking the truth . . . digging digging, digging. The truth about history, politics, art, literature. He was constantly reading and listening to others with differing opinions. There was usually a lively discussion going on at our table, since he had had such a wide-ranging and prolific career as a journalist.

In 1968 he started a movement in France, Americans Against the War in Vietnam. According to our friend and lawyer, Stanley Cohen, this movement had a big impact at the time. Jean opened up our house to deserters from Vietnam, who still had the privilege of entering France to seek refuge.

My father, who spoke in English like W. C. Fields, was absolutely unfathomable in French. My mother would even ask her granddaughter, Andrea, from time to time, "What did he say?" So Jean often had to translate for the workmen and engineers at Biémont, where my father's big structures, the stabiles, were built.

Jean was full of charm and humor, always ready to lend a helping hand. A great guy!

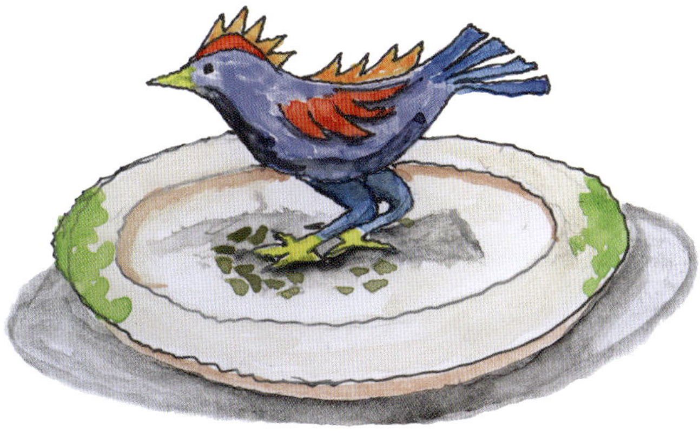

# Mary, Mary, Quite Contrary

Mary, my sister, and I were nearly four years apart and completely different—a daisy and a rose, two very different flowers grown from the same roots. The one thing we had in common all our lives was our parents. When Mary was born, I was thrilled to have a baby to care for. Being the eldest, I was the one who initiated the play plans when she grew older. My father installed a big blackboard in my room, which became the schoolroom. The students were Mary and our dog, Nero. We also played house for many years. I was the mother, and as far as I remember Mary was always ready to comply.

Then off to school you go and everything changes. As Mary was now alone with my parents and I was absent, she began to develop her own ways and swing her weight around, and assert her independence from me. Maybe that's why I started drawing her as a pig! A pig with a braid. She was very proud of her thick, long hair.

When Mary went to real school for the first time, it was a Catholic school in Aix-en-Provence. My mother and I drove over to pick her up in the afternoon, and as soon as she got into the car she burst into tears. When we got home, my father came out to see how the day had gone and bumped into three weeping females. That was the only day she attended that school.

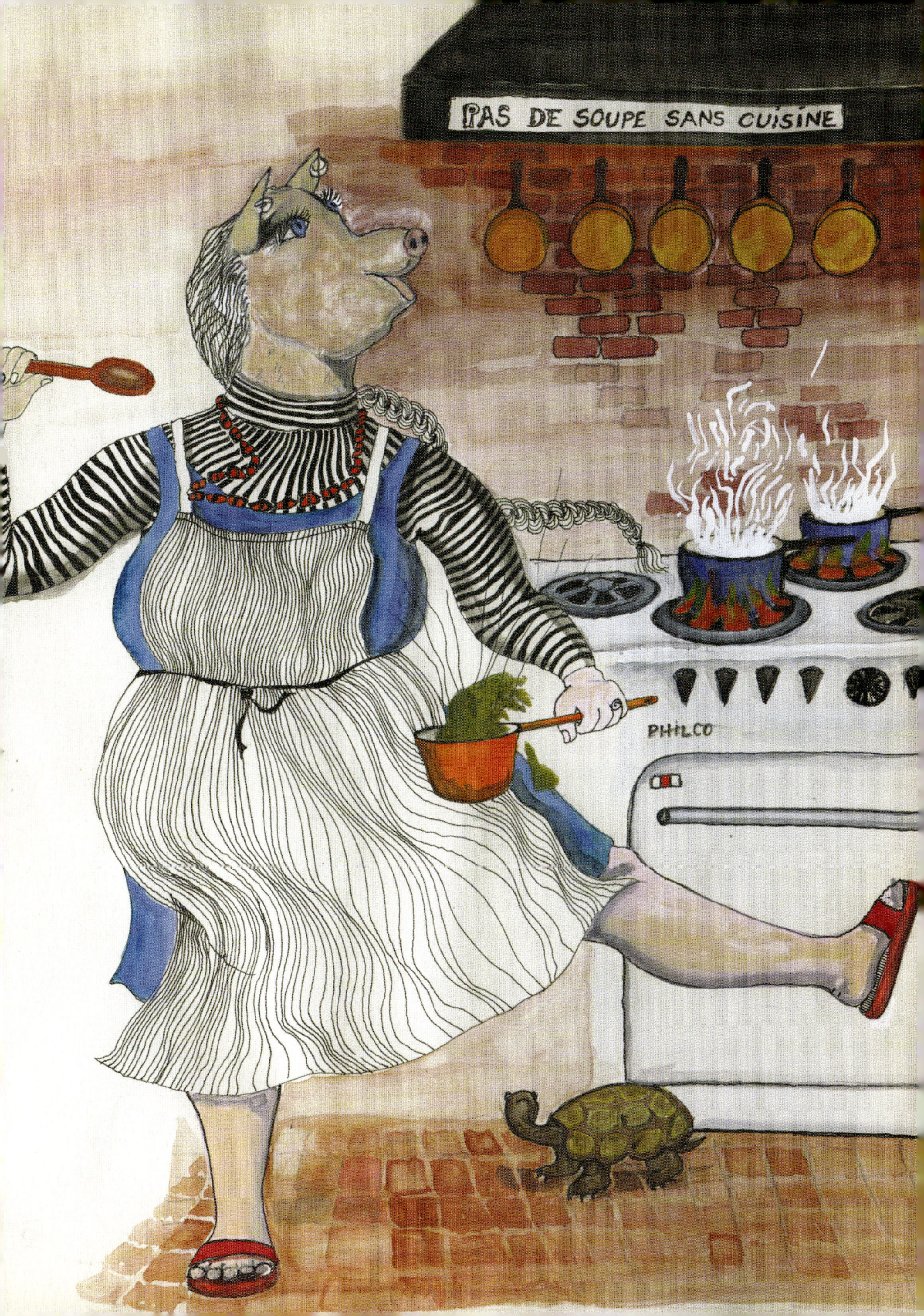
PAS DE SOUPE SANS CUISINE
PHILCO

# Mary, Mary, Quite Contrary

When we were twelve and fifteen respectively, I remember the screaming fights that took place in the elevator of the Madison Hotel, going down to breakfast. Our parents were waiting for us in the dining room, looking forward to a quiet meal. People could hear us all the way down to the basement. Mary reminded me of this some time ago. And of the time in Syria, when I jumped over the doorstep of a mosque and hit my head on the top of the doorframe, making such a loud bang that people stopped in their tracks to see who had just fired a shot. It was my head!

Then the husbands come along with their influences, good or bad. Now I was living in France with my husband, and Mary held her own in New York with her husband, Howard. They had many ongoing occupations and were always surrounded by people of all sorts. Influential people in the music world, in the cult world, and, because my parents were still in the States, in the art world. Mary loved to show me that I was a country bumpkin and knew nothing about the real world.

One morning in Paris, when we were both in our fifties and I had already lost Jean, we sat at a table on the terrace of a café with a few other friends. At one point during a moment of silence, Mary looked down at my watch and said, "I used to have a watch like that when I was eight years old!" I looked down at her Baume and Mercier Swiss grandfather clock that she had buckled around her wrist and noticed all the sub-dials telling her not only the time here and back home but the weather here and across the ocean, where she was expected for lunch, when she should move on back to the hotel. I looked down at my Pulsar, my watch intended for eight-year-olds, and saw that it was eleven a.m.

No matter how many blows we gave each other, there was always an underlying deep affection. We continued to enjoy the same basic pleasures in life: music, dancing, food, cooking, children. I will always be thankful to Mary for harboring my children when they left France, disgusted with the French school system, the lycée. I loved my sister and miss her terribly.

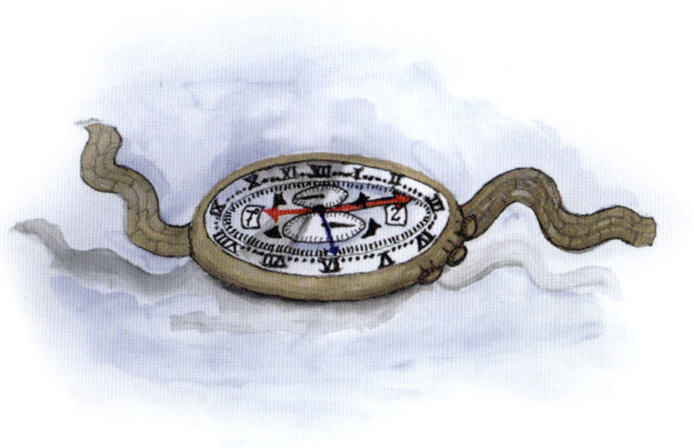

# Howard

George was the name of my brother-in-law Howard's parrot, and since I drew my brother-in-law as a parrot, I also named him after his own pet. Howard had many, many occupations and many projects all going on at the same time. Real estate—not the Madison Avenue type but buildings and apartments nonetheless: he had health food companies, clubs, restaurants. He was a collector of all sorts of objects, pieces from native peoples worldwide, from circuses, art galleries, and religious cults. He collected junk, piles of junk. I had to go to his office one day, and to make my way through the heaps of dentist chairs, doctors' desks, mechanics' benches, and car dealers' unsellables was a major task. You wedged your way through all of this sideways, inch by inch, grabbing onto elements that stuck out, like chair legs or couch arms, stovepipes, whatever. Finally, the office was in sight. There was George with his secretary, Anna, at the computer struggling to keep everything up and running.

Many people helped him in these endeavors. There were always people coming to or leaving MacDougal Street, wanting confirmation, seeking information, or going to dinner. I do think Mary loved the commotion. What would he have done without her? What would she have done without him?

Then the animals! Mary seemed to keep out of this scene. The animals were his hobby, and he had rabbits, tortoises, lions on the roof, chickens in the basement, sugar gliders, foxes, wolves, parrots, ferrets, and hedgehogs. Enough to fill a barnyard!

He certainly was eccentric, and now that I see him in memory many years later, I do think that all this turmoil was authentic. All these interests were part of who he was.

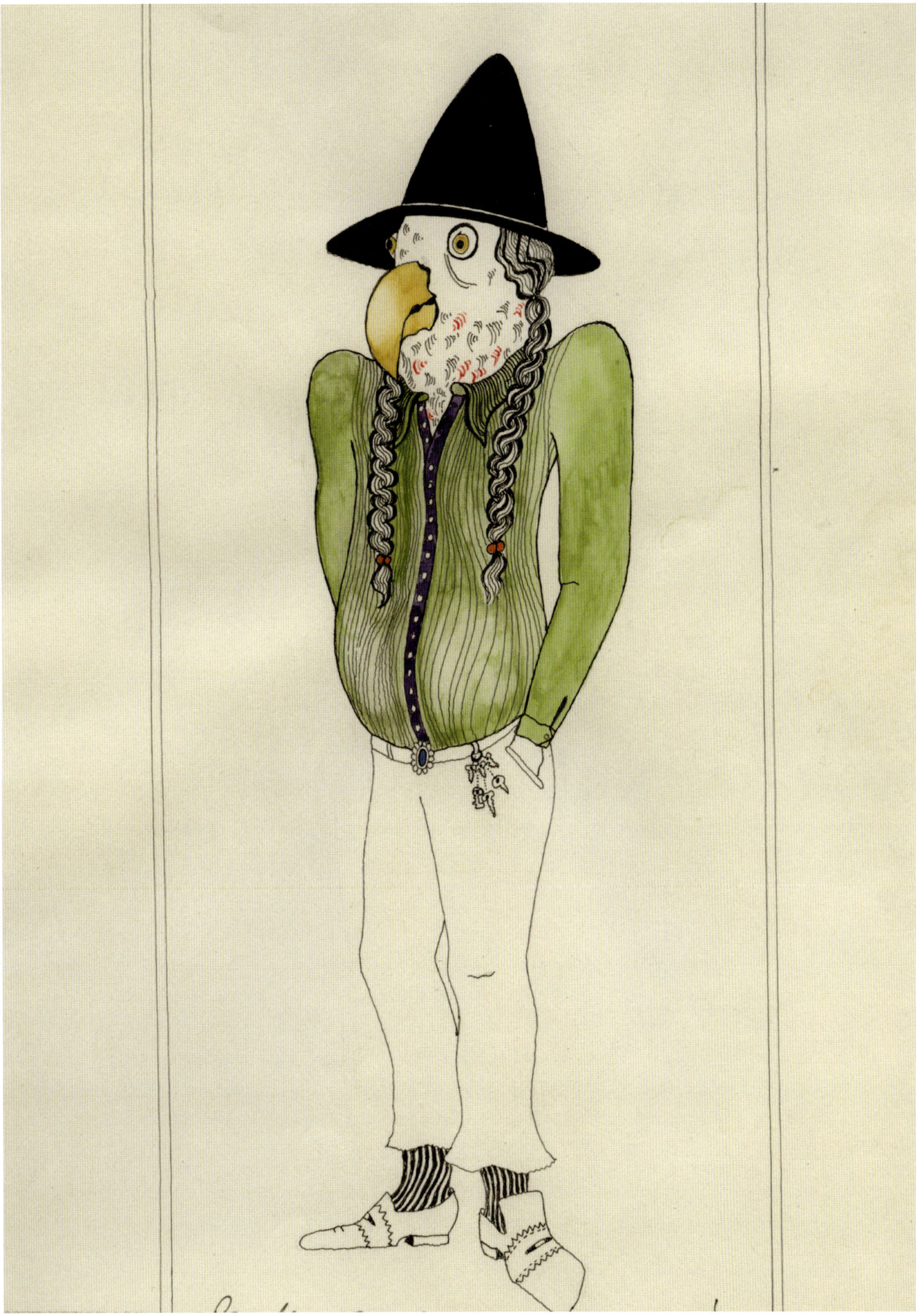

# Mary 2

As the years pass, it is the memories that hold you together. The bad moments dissipate, and, with the help of a therapist, you learn how to let the pricks and blows pass over your head like a flight of geese, maybe less noisy. You can now even laugh about all the events that you have undergone together. The two sisters with their opposite personalities, one bossy–Mary–and the other stubborn–me. Memories are the strings that keep us together, and the strings get longer as the years add up. And for heaven's sake, let the strings hang straight. Don't cut them with other purposes in mind. Strings are for binding, and the longer they are the closer they become.

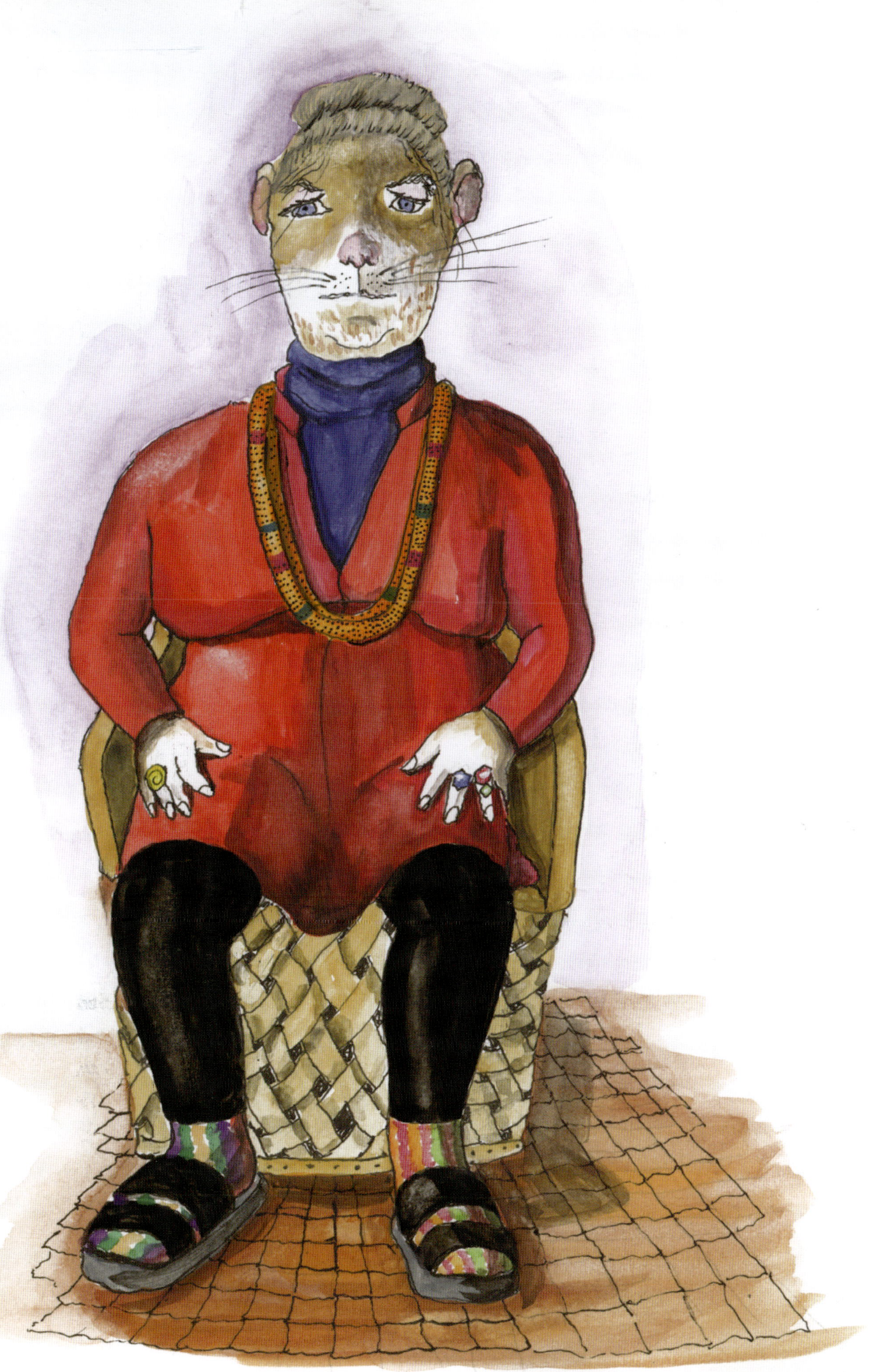

# Shawn

This long-legged giraffe is the biggest tease you ever did meet! He loves to pull people's legs, though his are much longer. I can only make out that he is a thinker—but a thinker who avoids making his thoughts available to others or showing his gentle, affectionate self.

When his sister, Andrea, was born, he received a box of lead soldiers given on her behalf. Most French boys had lead soldiers to play with at one point in their childhood. We hoped this present would reduce anxiety about having to compete with a sibling. While she was being bathed, he would command his soldiers around the room. Unfortunately, this present marked him in an unforeseen way, and he is now an ardent gun collector.

Boys don't feel the same demand to express themselves when they're babies and children as the girls do. That's too bad. Even if they do get the attention, society tends to squash that ability later on. For some reason, men are expected only to be heroes. We certainly have managed to bollix things up, us humans. To prove to themselves and others too that they're not only heroes but somehow loving fathers as well, some men will be seen pushing the baby carriage on Saturdays and Sundays.

Shawn's ongoing studies, among others of the Russian language, led him to Russia, where he found the love of his life. I do believe that he speaks his mind to his Russian friend, if for no other reason than to exercise his language skills.

Shawn, the giraffe, is the big mystery man. He's a mystery to his mother, to the mason, to the roofer, to the carpenter, and to his sister. I must say that being a mystery leaves you a lot of leeway.

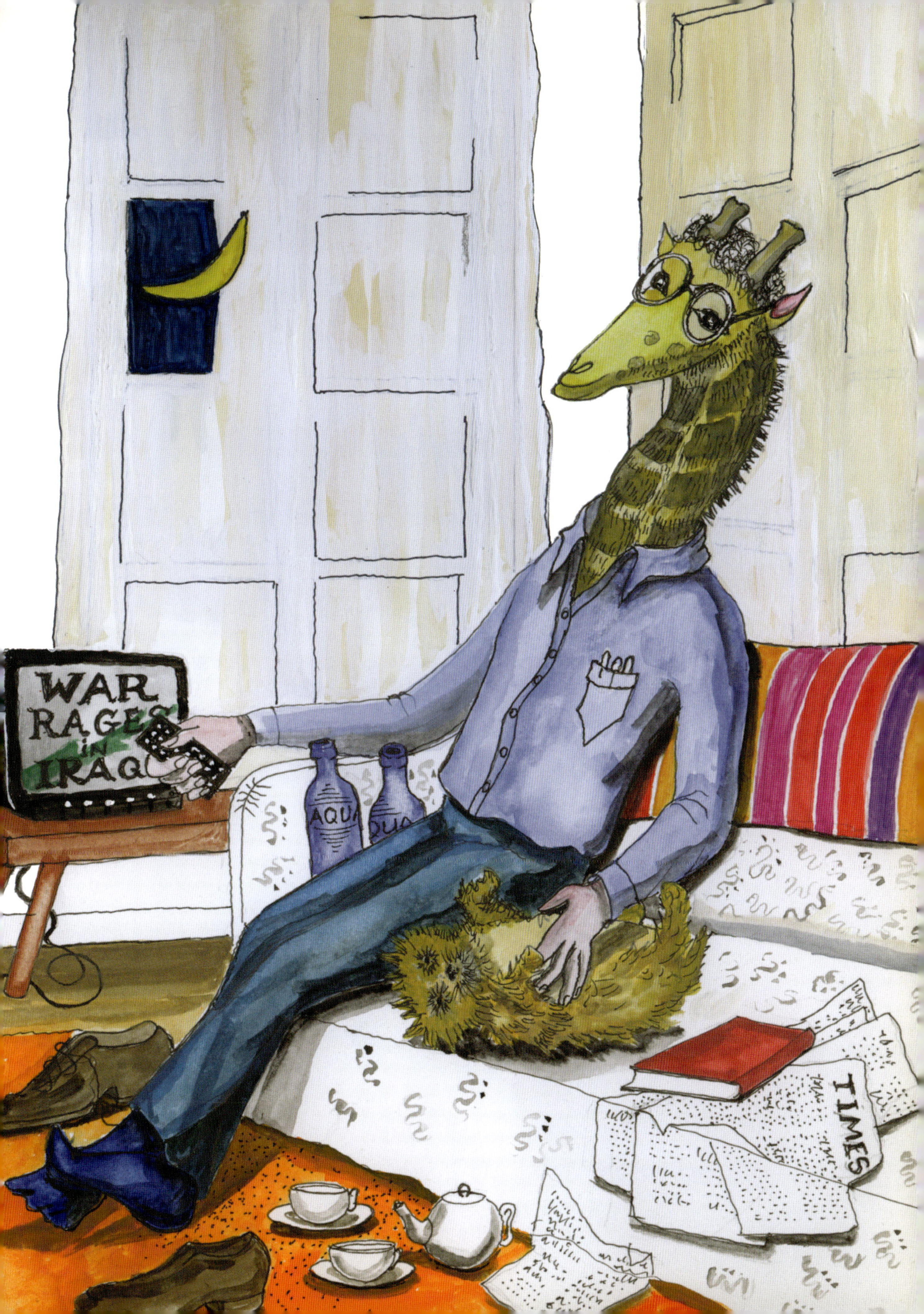
WAR RAGES in IRAQ
AQUA
TIMES

# My Andrea

This is my Andrea, my personal eclectic surprise ball, like the crystal ball that falls from the sky every New Year's Eve in New York! Only, in this case, I'm the one who falls from the sky. She has never settled for a dull day! When the lights start flashing and the cymbals clash and the whistles blow and the sirens sound, my heart beats hard and I hold my breath.

She has traveled; she has met all kinds and types. She lends an open ear to all and then moves on. The crystal ball is full of precious items. Paintings! Dresses (she was a seamstress)! Needlework! Tapestries! Mosaics! Lawsuits! Boyfriends! Friends! Dogs! Most of them saved from the poor house or the streets. Broken bones! Medical bills! Chronic diseases! And at last . . . Joachim!

She is beautiful, disheveled, brilliant, an excellent mother. Some call her Hurricane Harriet. I call her Totrey!

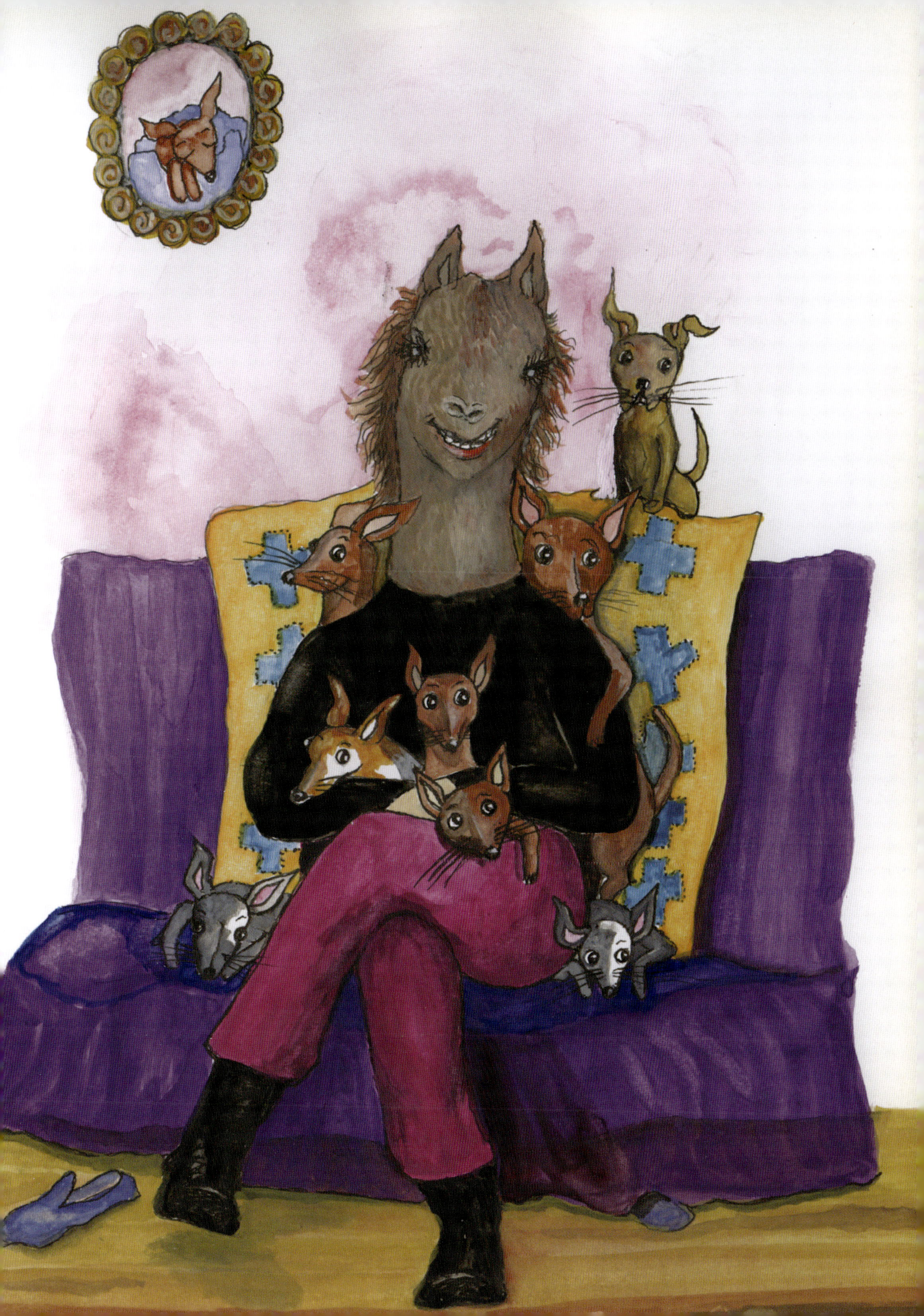

# Anya

My precious and flamboyant granddaughter and my son's very special daughter. Strangely enough, they resemble each other in character in their secretiveness. She, unlike my son, never has a minute to spare except for her stray dogs. She might even prefer stray dogs to pompous people. Like the rest of us, she doesn't like pomp. That is a trait that goes all the way down the line. She is self-dressed, self-styled, self-coiffed, and is always an elegant one-of-a-kind. She has, as one might expect, a single-mindedness, a single stroke. A singular approach to her work as an illustrator. She is mine too, and we have very recently realized how well we empathize.

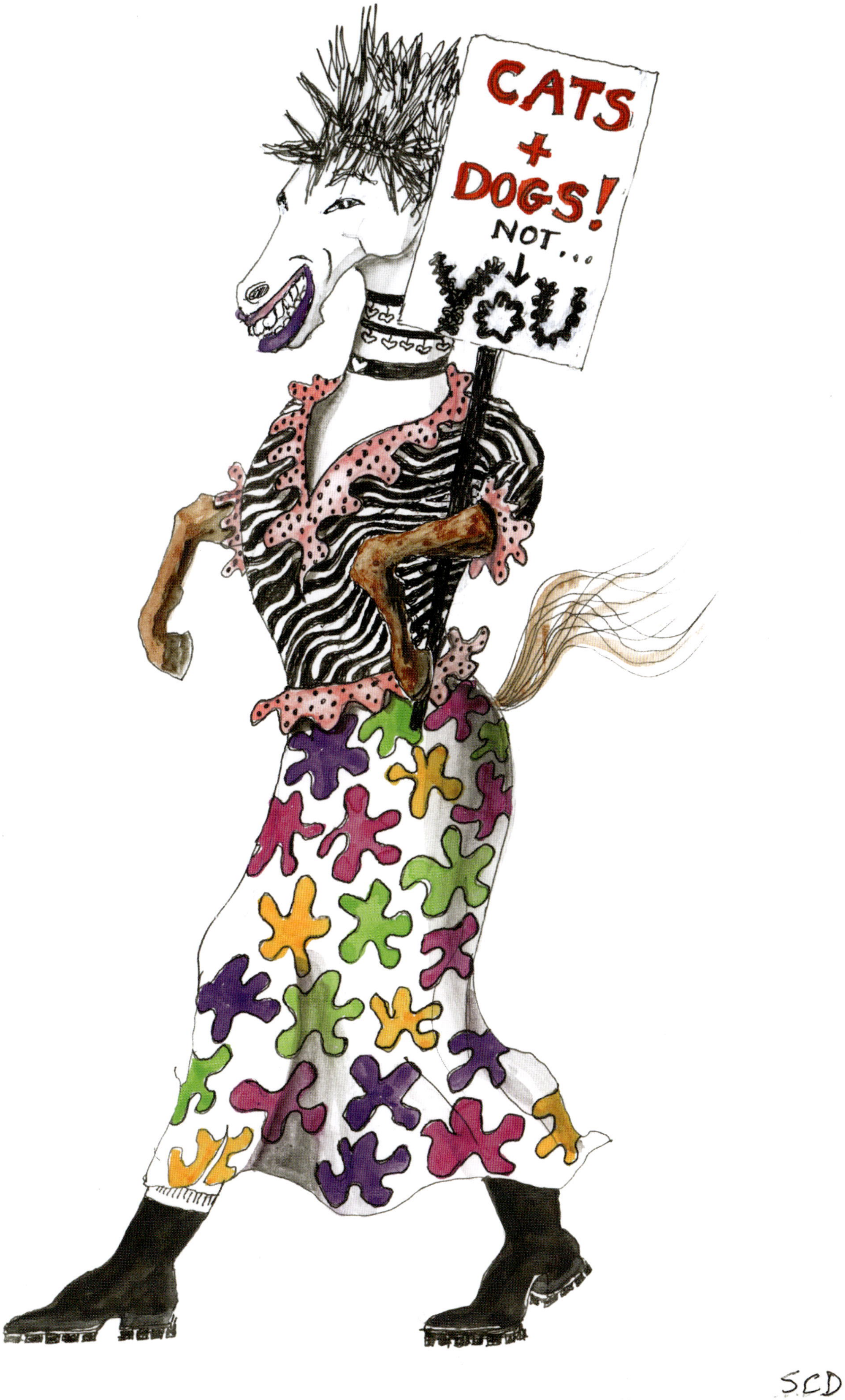
CATS
+
DOGS!
NOT...
YOU
SCD

# Joachim

Here he is, Joachim, my grandson, the only one you'll see with a human face. That's because they are human until we teach them all the devilish things that we do and think. Children are so intelligent, so thoughtful, so loving and non-discriminatory. They don't care if you're short or tall, thick or thin, black or white. They don't care if you look like a squirrel or a turtle. They just know that there's a lot to be learned from a squirrel or a turtle and a lot to give them. They are not riddled with ideas about who is to be looked down upon.

You get saddled with these feelings as time goes on. They have no notions of who's right and who's wrong, or of giving lessons: Do this, do that. I suggest you see the movie *Babies*, if you want to know what I mean.

It's remarkable how these small creatures learn to grow anywhere, in the desert of Africa or the plains of Mongolia. I would love to see these babies all together in a wide open space with their mothers not far off.

So this Joachim is very open to people. He likes to listen, and he likes to share. In school the children come to get him if there is an argument to be settled. He loves the water, and he loves to fish. For the time being, he is mostly physical–sports, skateboarding, and walking. He is great company, and I have the hunch that he will have a great deal to give to humanity. He will excel in whatever he decides to do, and somehow I think he will remain as open and giving as he is now.

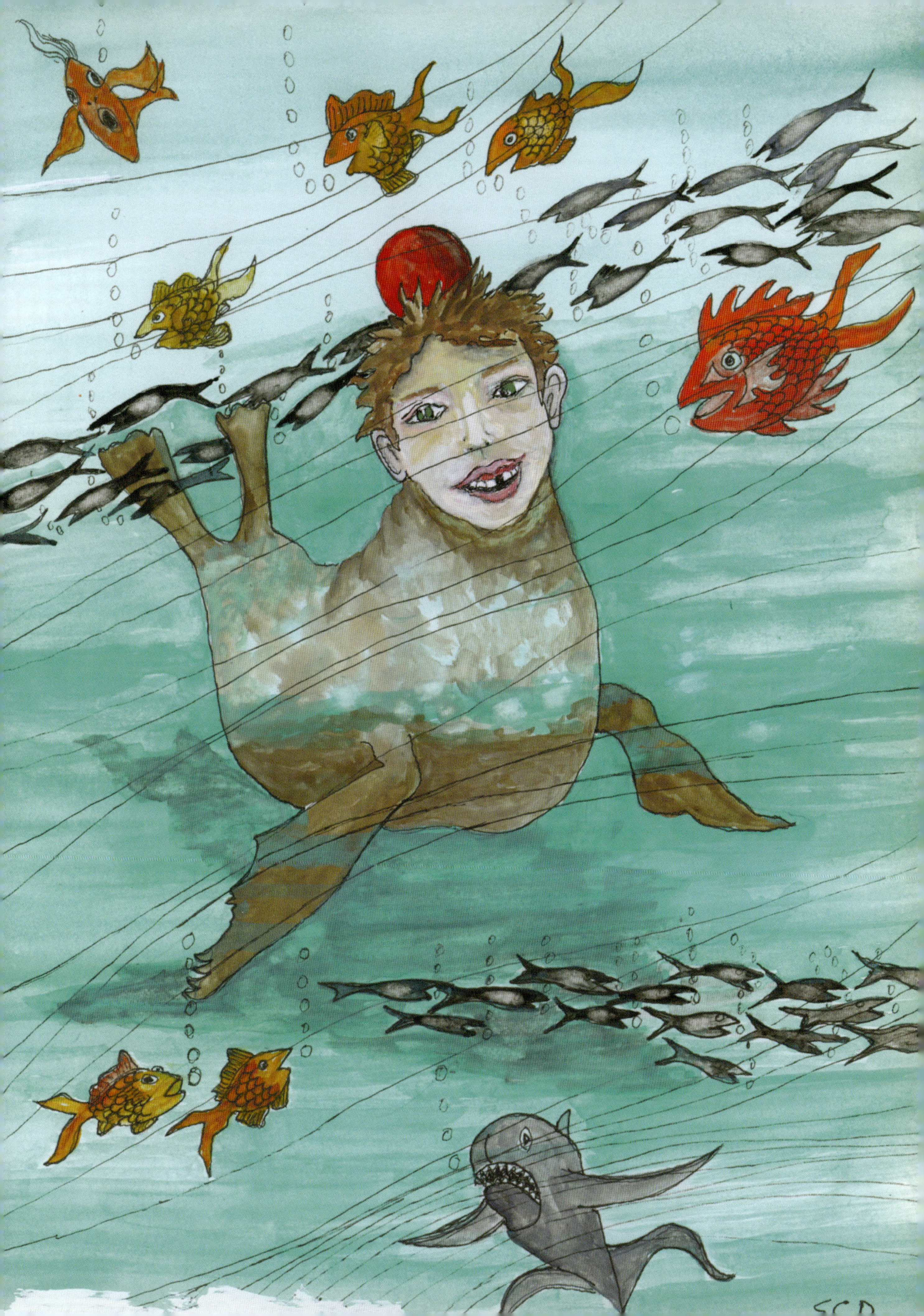

# The Boys

They went from adorable at six months to cute until about four years old, then fresh until about ten years old, then smartasses through the teens, maybe later. Normal, I guess. We lived on two continents, and a summer visit was a must so that everyone might see where the devils were at. My parents' house was next-door, which provided the necessary back and forth space. I guess they got along with Andrea and Shawn. I never asked anyone. Then, all of a sudden, one was missing, off to school. Then another, off to camp . . . Then yours goes . . . and how dreadful is that? Then one gets married, another takes a trip with a boyfriend. The boyfriend Fred turns into Don without any notice. The third one has a baby, the fourth goes to Israel to raise chickens, and pretty soon there's no telling who's doing what. Then a young lady comes up to you and says, "Hey, Auntie!," and you know that that young lady has to be a great-niece.

Hey! Wait a minute. I was an aunt just a short time ago! Now I'm a great-aunt, and during all this time you are wondering what the hell you are supposed to be doing with the last half of your life, empty of all these rovers on the go.

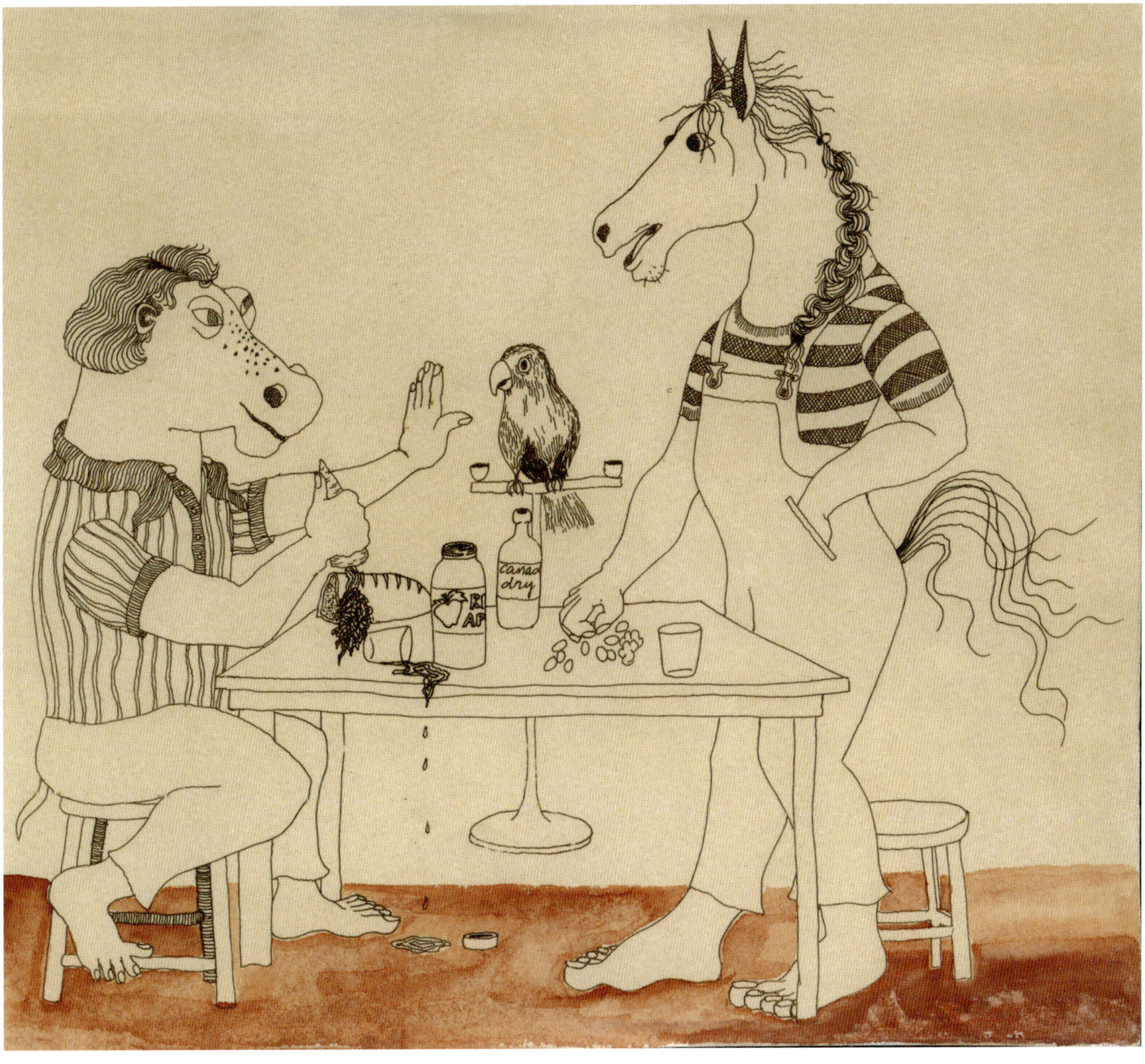
RI
AP
canad
dry

# Sandy

We have all moved onward in age, in experience, in preconceived ideas, in new ideas, and in lifestyles. We all, I mean "the family," have great admiration, I think, for what my father (Sandy's grandfather) accomplished. We all live off of what he accomplished, but Sandy has been the force, the unrelenting force behind the foundation. It is a remarkable institution, run with precision and passion. I can't, and do not want to imagine what would have happened if he had not taken over.

Here he is, Monsieur le Directeur, Alexander Stirling Calder Rower, head of the Calder Foundation, who knows how to swim in the murky waters of the twenty-first century Art World.

The first lesson he gives is: "Gently does it!" You don't have to hit a mobile with an umbrella, or give it a whack with your arm, to get it to move. A gentle whisper or a small flurry or a tiny puff will put every branch into movement. A flurry that is one of a kind. It will never, but never, swing that way again.

Thank you, Sandy, for taking your job so seriously!

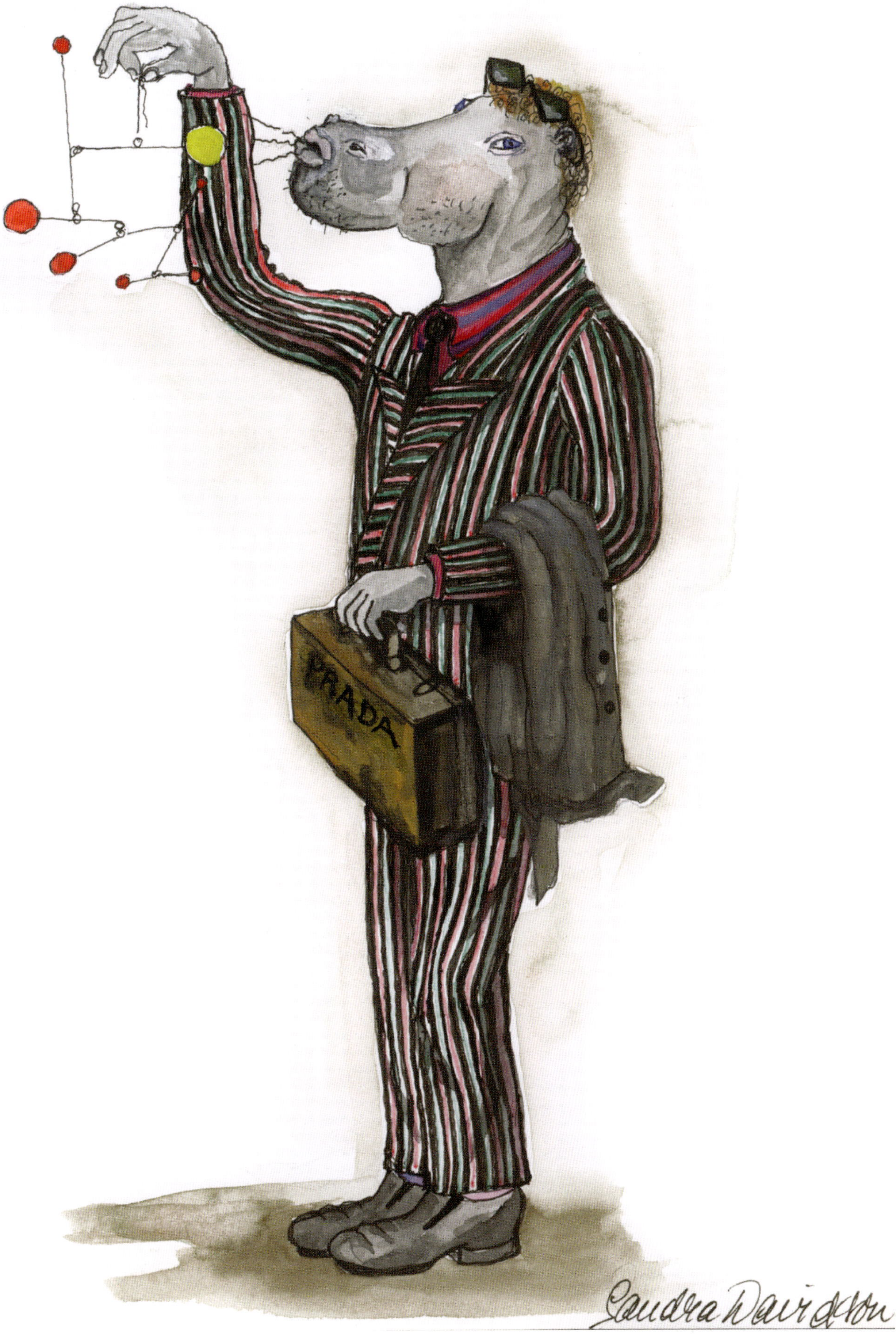
PRADA
Sandra Davidson

# Saul Steinberg

Saul Steinberg said, "It's hard to do a portrait. You must first spend a critical moment in which you quickly—if you're lucky—discard the commonplaces about the subject of the drawing. More difficult than inventing is giving up accumulated virtues. The things you discovered yesterday are no longer valid. It's impossible to find anything new without first giving something up."

I knew Saul as a friend of the family. I liked him a lot. We never had any discussions about drawing, which I regret, for to me he is one of the best, one of the major illustrators we've had. And behind the drawing, with all its humor, is a deep-seated philosophy.

He appeared to be very serious and very observant . . . a quiet fellow. My portraits are simply a congregation of different symptoms once I've discarded the commonplaces about the subject. I do hope he would have liked his portrait.

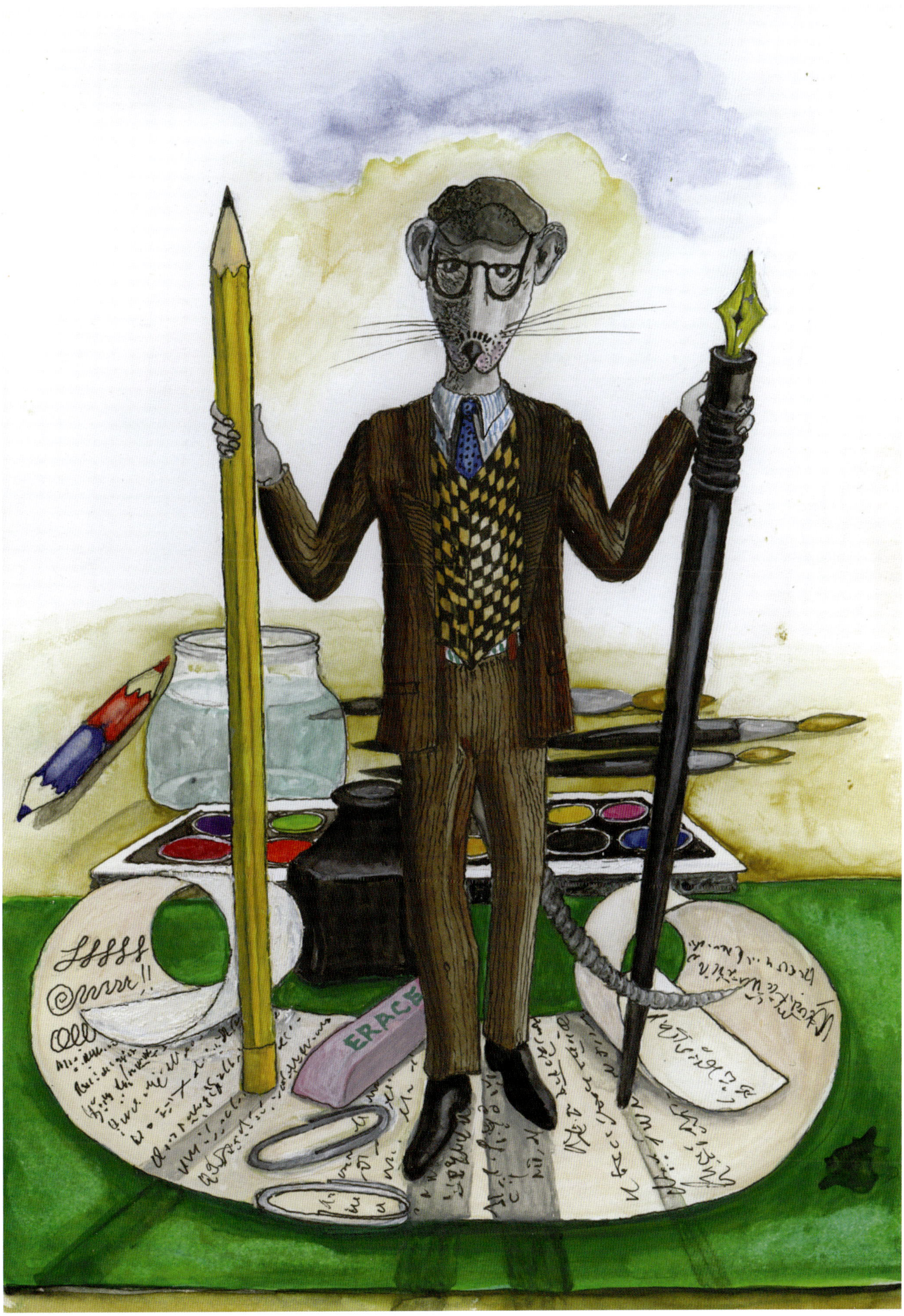
ERACE

# Arthur Miller

Arthur Miller was our next-door neighbor, and I enjoyed his and Inge's company. We were all on the same page politically. I never really saw him that much, though. I was away at school, and then I went to live in France. He wrote a very good and humorous piece about my father in *Calder in Connecticut.* I am just going to cite a bit of that:

> Sandy would not want moralizing about his life. But there is no way to avoid mentioning one aspect of his character. He was not a judgmental man—not at all. I do not know a couple who had friends of such a wide variety of opinions and convictions. He, like Louisa, was nevertheless committed, and it expressed itself in sometimes public statements on the Vietnam war and other issues. But important as these were, they symbolized the real commitment that I have always thought was to human decency.

I'm glad Arthur felt that way. So did I.

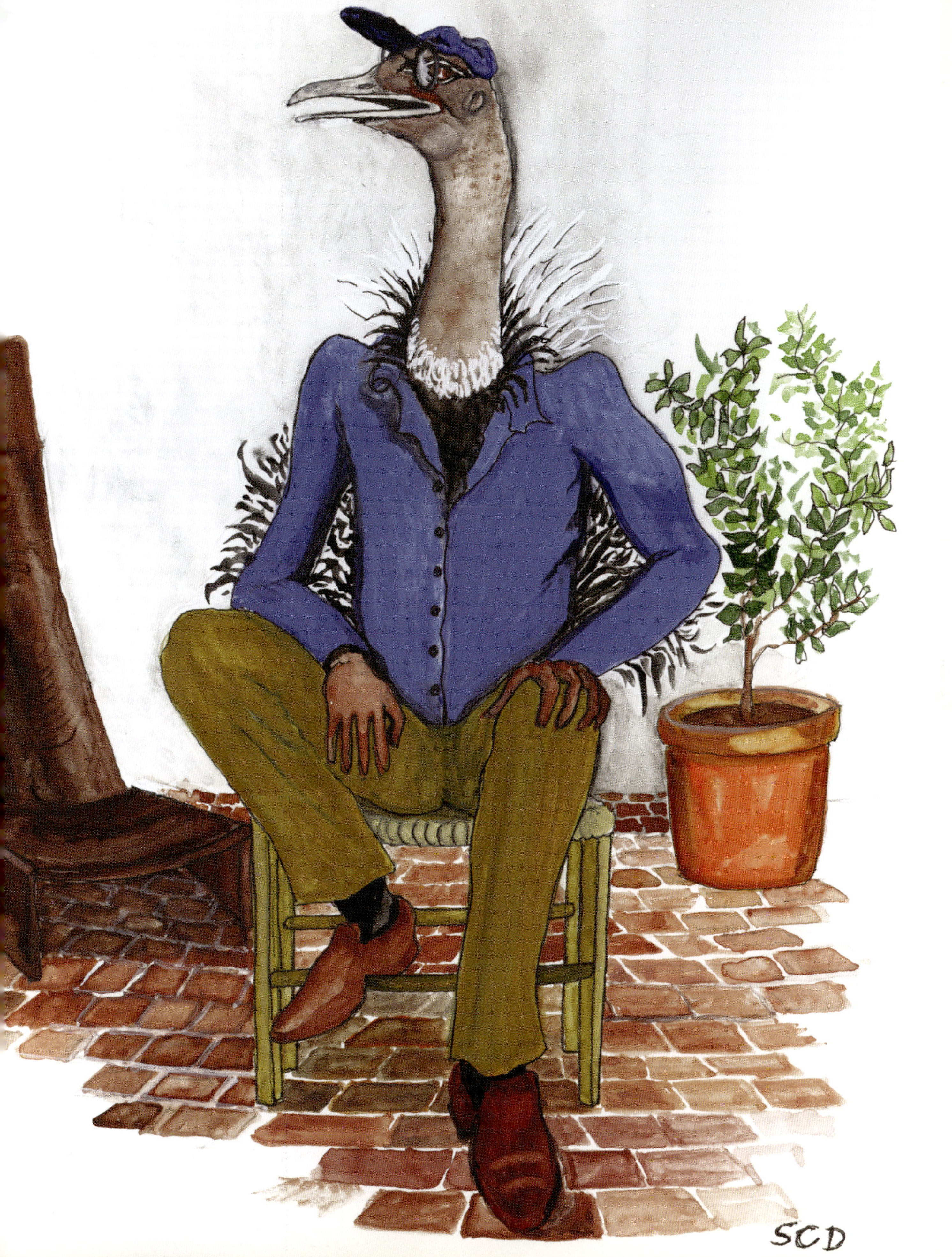
SCD

# The Rocker McClintock

Back on the Brittany coast, the rocker Michael McClintock doesn't really need his shades. It must be a habit. It must be a habit that rockers have. Not only rockers, by the way: politicians, movie stars, thugs, Mafioso share it too. Sunny or stormy, to keep out the glare, so they say, but in truth to keep you from looking in. For, you see, there is a direct line from the regard of your eyes to the center of your soul.

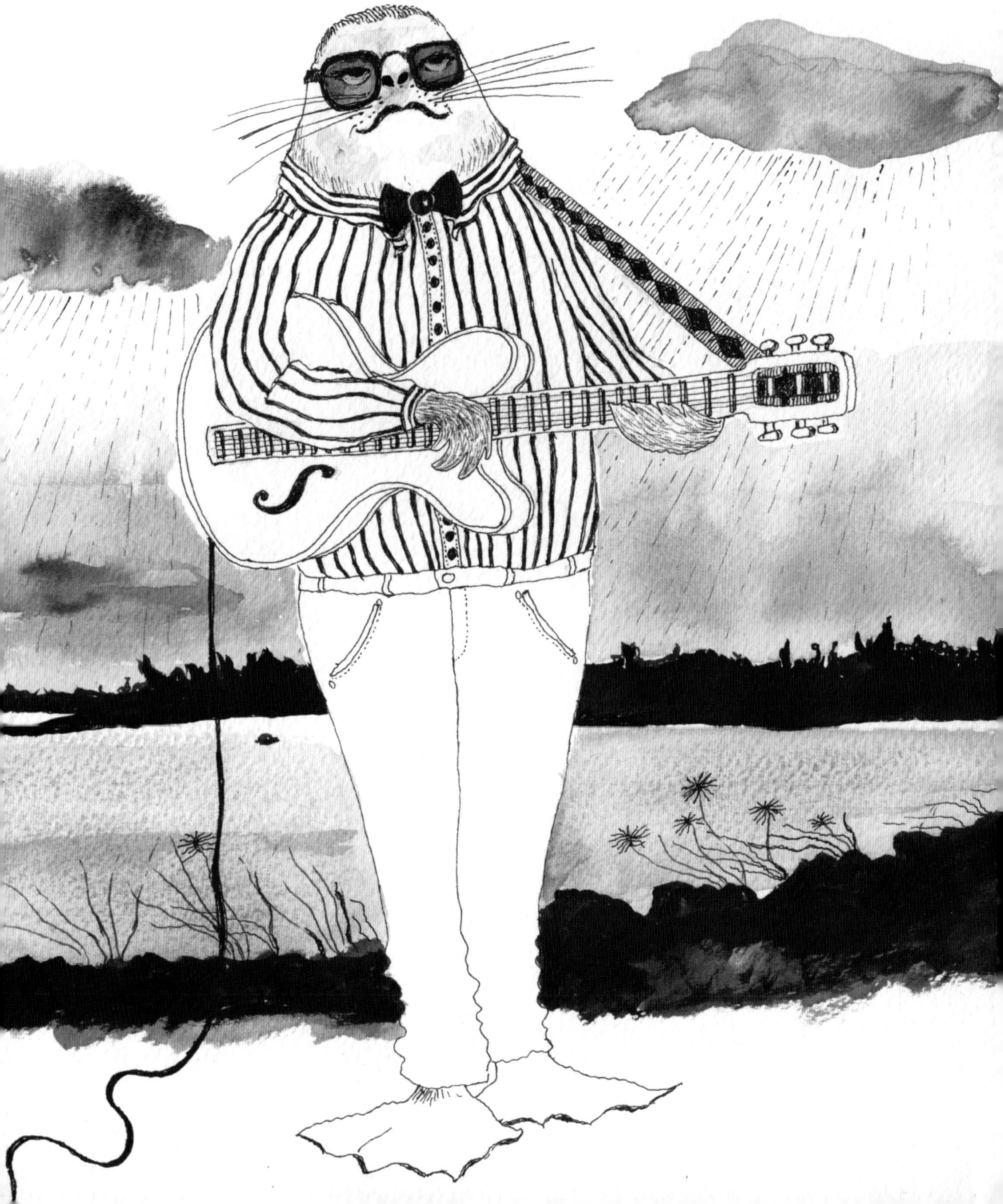

# Sylvain

Wired up and ready to go! That's Sylvain's rhythm of life. As though he had been wound up with a key like a toy. Big steps, ready to go! Always with determination. Not in a rush, but on the move. Key also means pitch. He is a musician, a violinist. A very good violinist, the first violin I could ever listen to. My grandfather had a violin, a Stradivarius. He had cut off the neck to see what other sounds he could obtain. I had already done a portrait of him, as a grandfather, not as a critter, with his violin when I was about eight years old. The sound he obtained was atrocious. It was many years later that I listened to Sylvain play his. I have no idea what the make of his instrument is. He no doubt has several. I never, but never, thought a violin could bring such music to my ears!

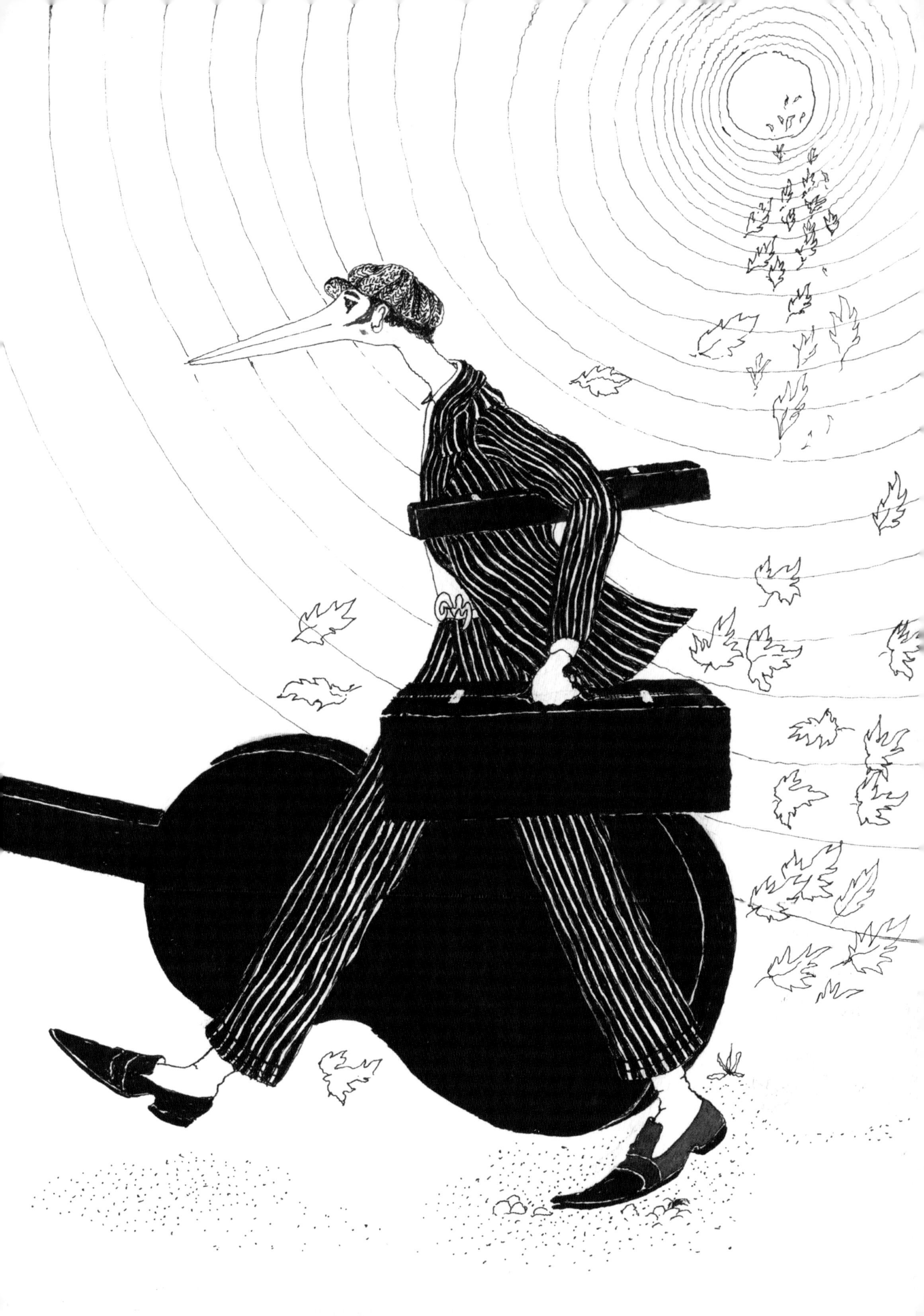

# The Girls of New York, Circa 1970

Some like them stout, some like them thin, all like them hot!

The girls of New York are in a tough spot.

Should I wear polka dots?

Should I wear squares?

A tight dress, or a dress that flares?

It's impossible to say,

For what's true today

Tomorrow is passé:

For a fashion queen

Every day is Halloween!

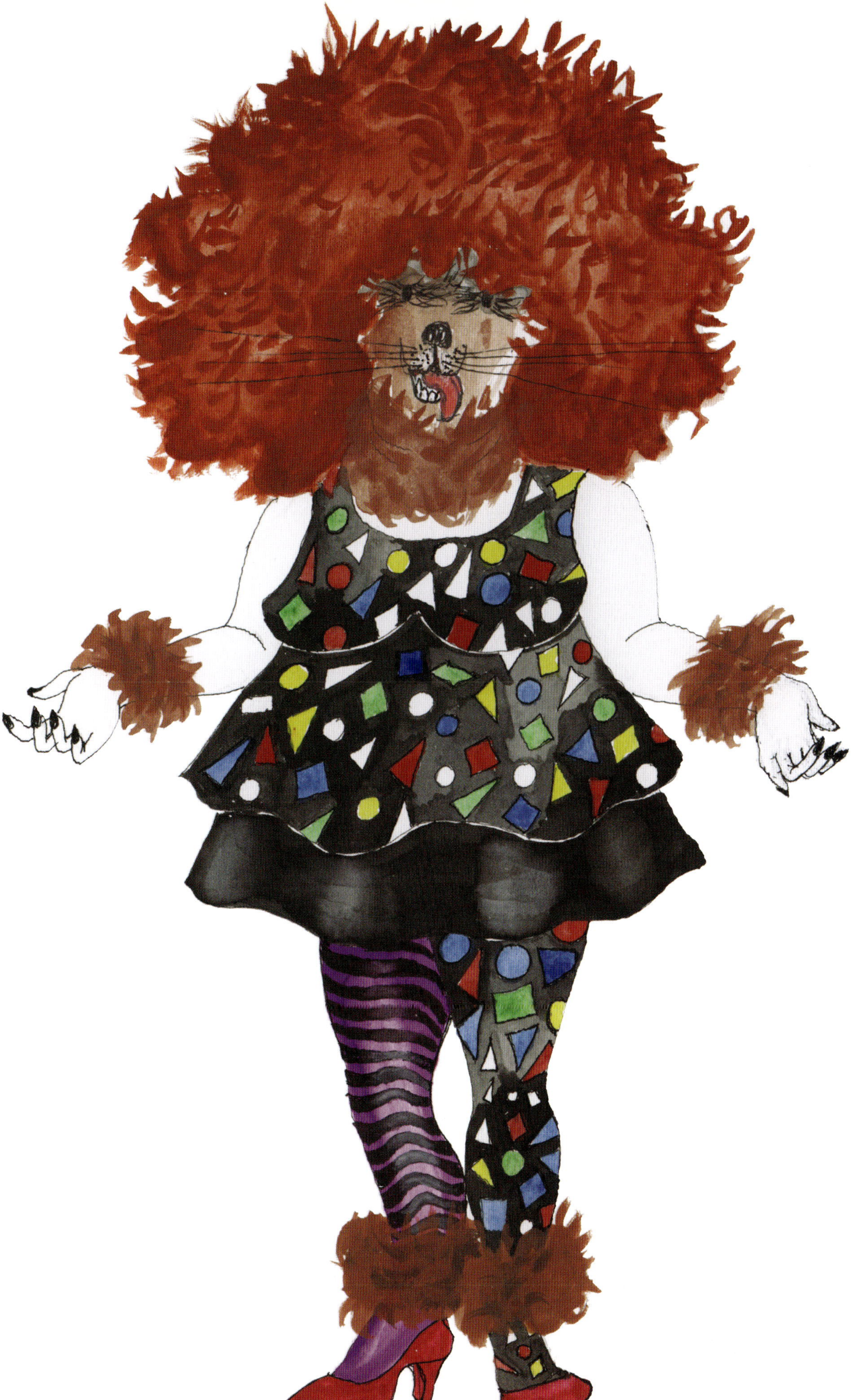

# The Present-Day Girls of New York

The heels of the shoes that the young ladies of New York wear nowadays are so high they might as well be called Eiffel Towers in reverse. Between those tall towers and the crumbling streets of New York there have been many a twisted ankle and even a broken one, God forbid. But these girls are courageous and continue to stride along at a slow pace. It's true—from time to time they grab hold of their boyfriend's arm to regain their balance. Frankly, I don't understand how they do it after a night out on the town!

The girls of New York have other things to worry about too. Such as the humongous diesel trucks three sidewalks long that circulate in the city, spitting out deadly fumes in everyone's faces. The girls stroll their babies in carriages that hold them at exactly exhaust-pipe level. Think about it, girls of New York!

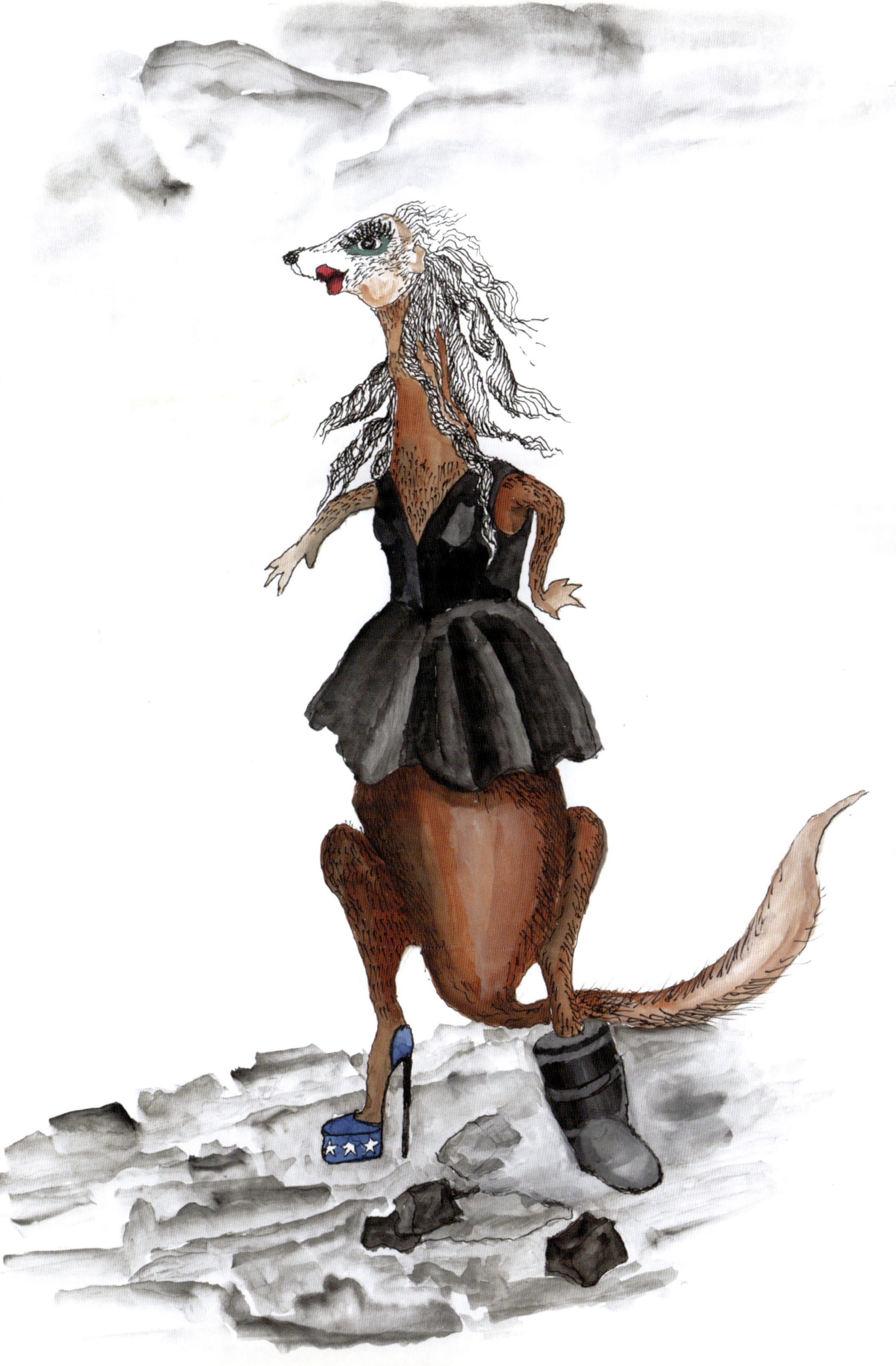

# Jeannette and Suzanne

These girls both came from different parts of the Republic of Chad. They speak French as their native language. They met at an English class in midtown Manhattan and now both speak broken English too and have jobs taking care of Barbara, Lucile, and John. They meet in Central Park after breakfast and walk the babies, so that later the children will take long naps. They tell each other about their past lives, about how they got out of Chad and how they managed to get to the U.S. They also discuss their respective families. American culture and the culture of Chad could not be more different. So when there is a misunderstanding between the parents and a nanny, Jeannette can always confide in Suzanne or the other way around.

Luckily, there are these immigrants, for what would we do without them?

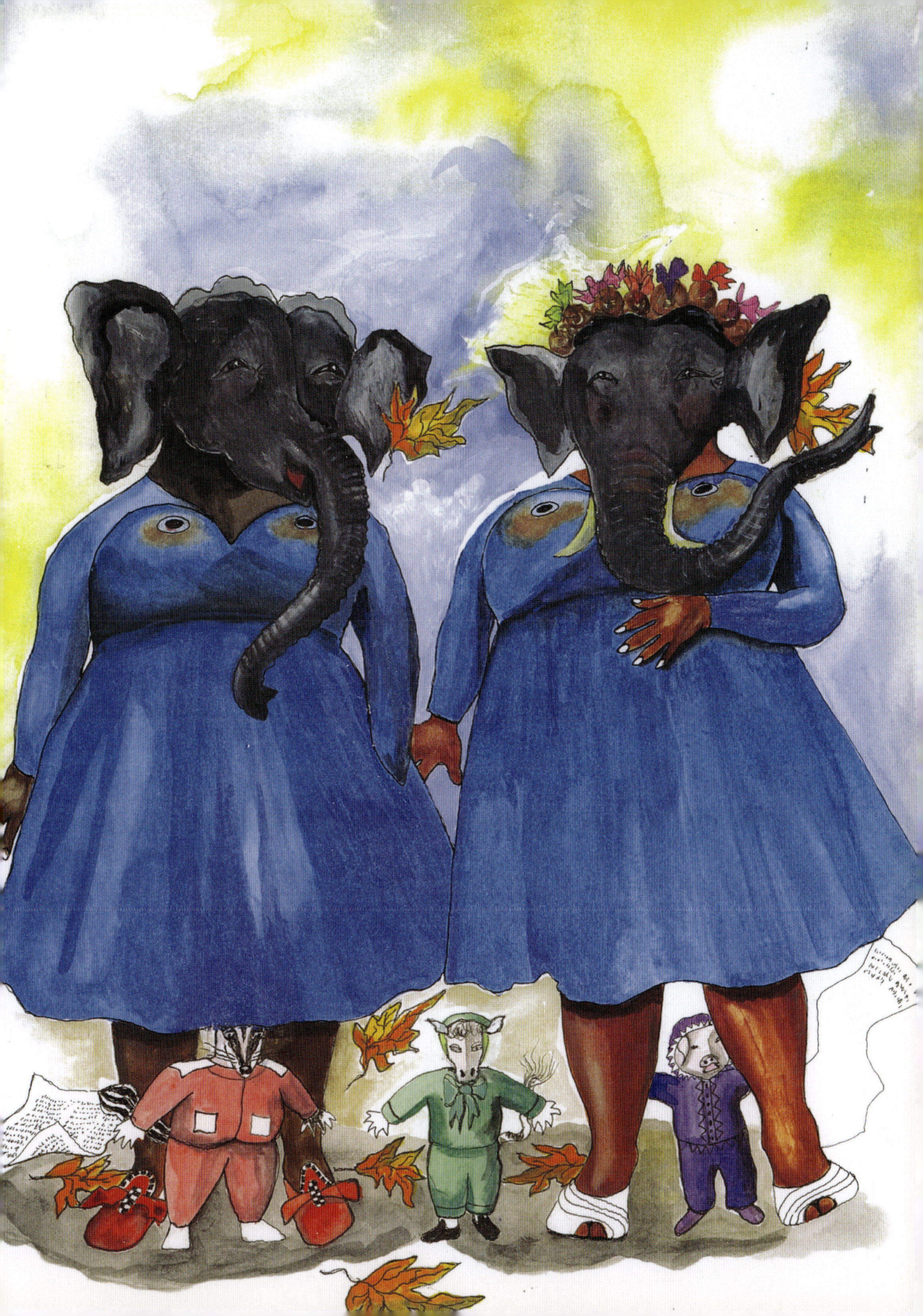

# Peter Hyun

This Korean friend I met in Paris many years ago. I had just finished school and had decided to stay in France when my parents left. I had no idea what Peter did or what he was doing there. He spoke perfect English and perfect French. Had it been nowadays, I would have wondered more deeply . . . what with spies having become a fact of life. Things seemed to be so easygoing in those days, or is it that I was just ignorant? Then we lost touch for many years, until he met my parents through Arthur Miller. He was now working at Doubleday and was eager to publish my first children's book, *Sylvester, the Lead Frog,* which he did, and the second one, too. We have met off and on throughout the ages. Now he and his wife, Young Yi, live in so many different countries I can't keep up. Here he is on the bridge to Somewhere.

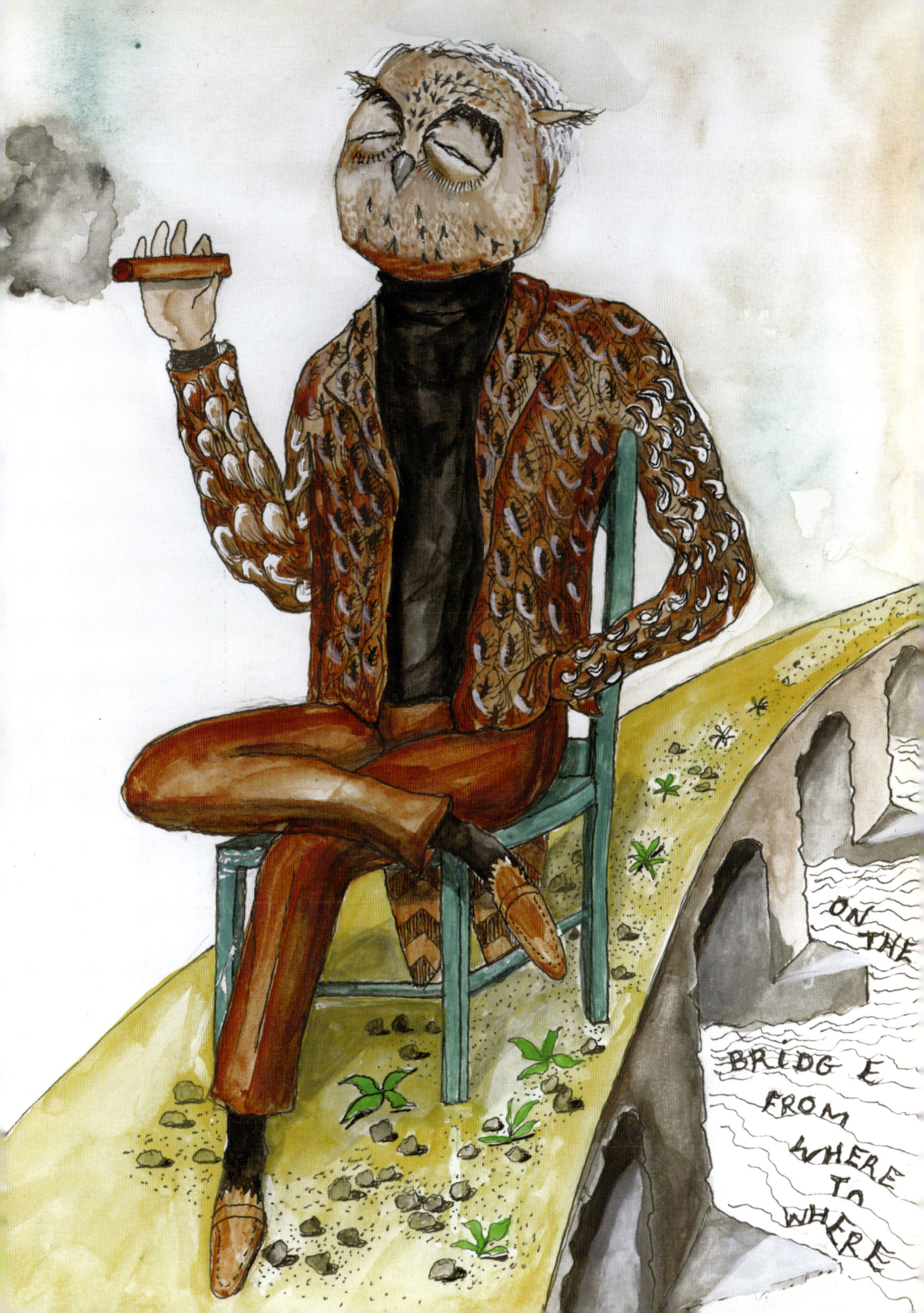
ON THE
BRIDG E
FROM
WHERE
TO
WHERE

# Sean Sweeney

Please meet my friend, the dapper Sean Sweeney.

Friends for three generations deep. I sent him his portrait rather than give it to him. I was afraid he might want to use his tusks on me. One can't always be sure of what one draws, or how it will be received. But then, you don't do someone who has no humor. Anyway, he wrote me back, saying that "the tusks are perfect. The more respectable walruses I saw in Greenland had yellow tusks. The more respectable, the yellower." Yes, that word "respectable" describes Sean Sweeney perfectly. He has lived in India, Saudi Arabia, Iran, Japan, Greenland, Iceland, and of course his native Ireland. He speaks twenty-five languages. Besides his respectability and his knowledge, he is also notable as the one and only trustee of the James Joyce estate. Sean told me about a very famous portrait painter who was sent over to do a portrait of Joyce. As Joyce posed, the painter tried to make his painting as resemblant and meaningful as possible.

"I would like to understand your mind," the painter said to Joyce.

"Forget about my mind," said Joyce to the painter. "Make sure you get my tie straight!"

"So," said Sean to me, "thank you for my fine hat and overcoat!"

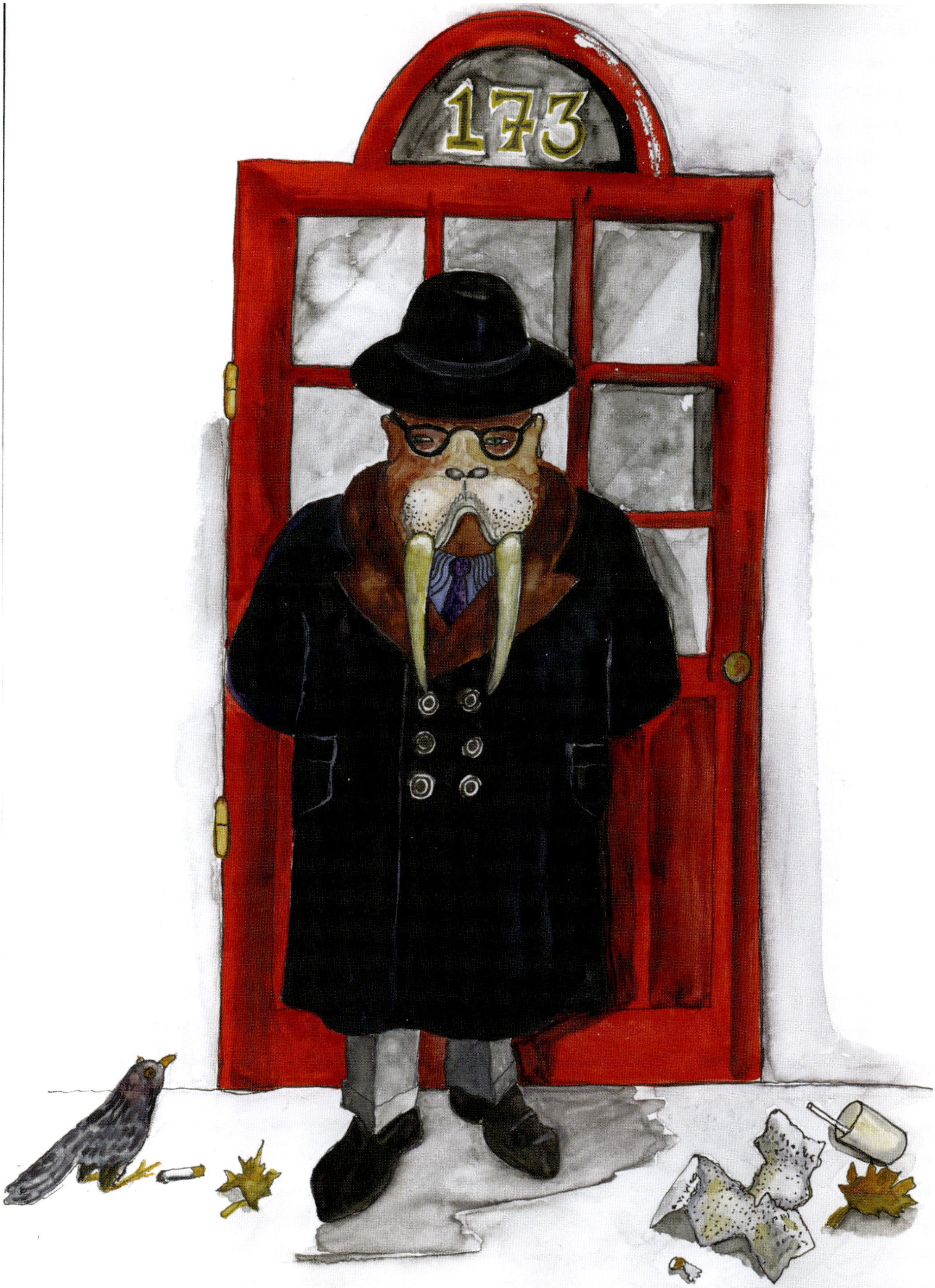
173

# Pink Fluff

I descended the steep Rhinecliff station steps holding on tight to the rail and looked out over the Hudson River. But something caught my eye on the platform. A shocking sight! A woman all dressed in pink, and to top that off she had bright red hair. Her sneakers were pink, and her bag was pink. Her cheeks had a thick coating of pink powder.

My father years ago warned us how much he hated the color pink. I understood then that it was quite an obsession. Which meant, to me, that we had better beware. Now I tore my eyes away from this pink monster and tried to concentrate on the river. I descended the steps keeping my distance and tried to make out if the tide was coming in or going out.

"Excuse me!" said an anxious voice close to me. "Have you taken this train before?"

"Yes, I have, many times," I tried to reassure her. The color pink had already taken on an off-pink coloring, and instead a troubled lady stood next to me.

"I am on my way to Washington, D.C.," she explained. "I am going to a symposium of top Alzheimer's specialists of the country. Both my son and my husband are afflicted with this terrible disease. I am going to tell them all that I know."

Here was this little woman going off to unknown parts, hoping no doubt that she might make a particle of difference in the search for a cure. And here I was, standing next to her worrying about the color of her outfit!

What did I know about the color pink? How did that obsession of my father's manage to make its way into my subconscious? I felt like a perfect fool.

Soon Amtrak came chugging along. I sat down in one of those comfortable seats, hoping never to have such a reaction again.

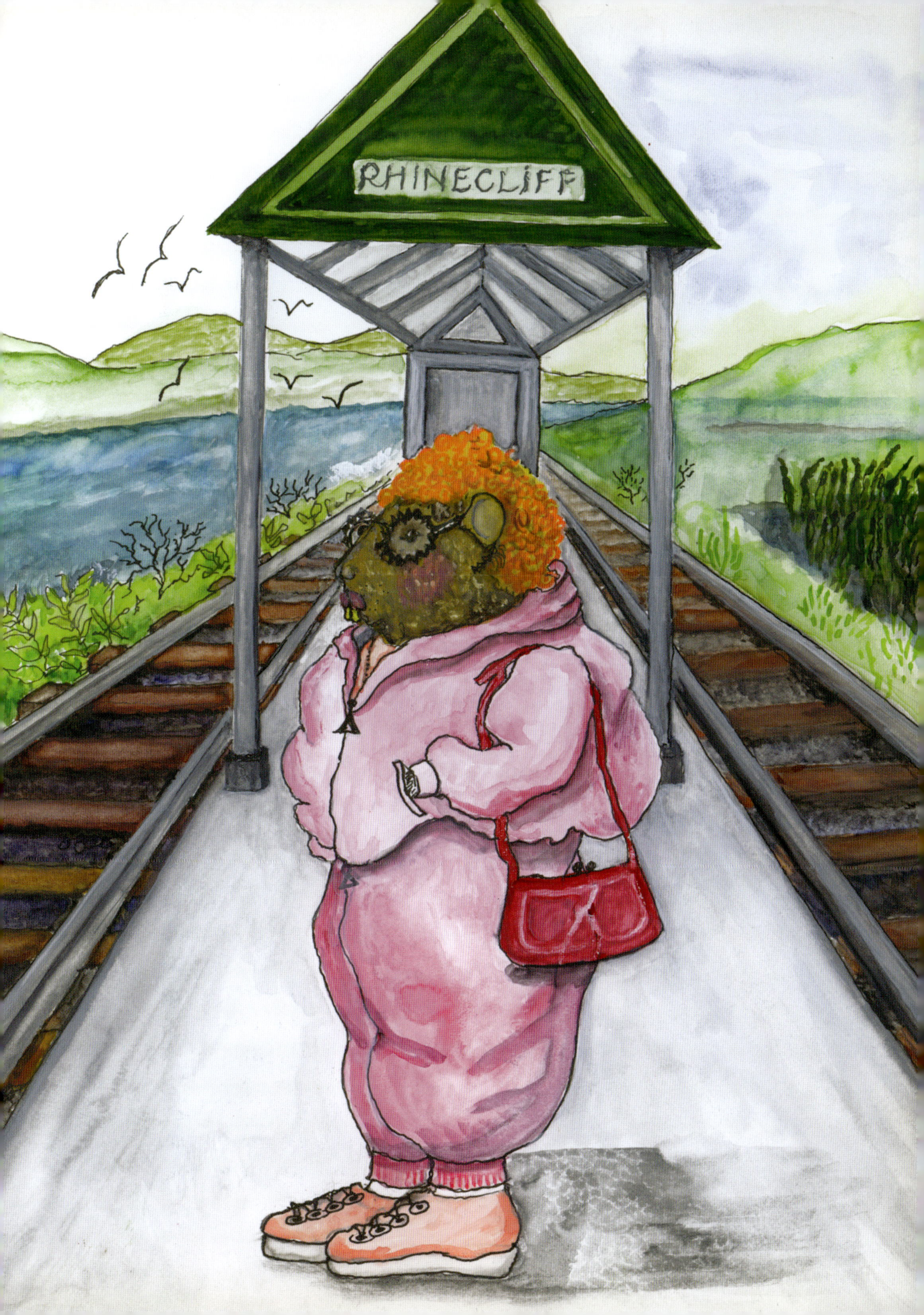
RHINECLIFF

# Kika

Kika and I have known each other throughin and throughout our lifetimes. Our mothers were best friends, and our fathers were too. (Her mother was Ritou Bac; her father was the architect Oscar Nitzschke.) They all had good times in the cafés around town, in Paris and New York. Everyone liked to cook, and everyone liked to eat and drink. I didn't have to be embarrassed by my parents, because hers were much the same. She spent most of her time reading, while I played with dolls. She is slow moving. She turns everything over in her head until she's sure she's got it right. One can never be too sure.

She dreams and savors. She wonders about measures she has to take, like it or not, turning them inside out and upside down, then tilting to the left and to the right. One never knows if one is doing the right thing anyway, particularly when it comes to three daughters. Her cats are much easier to make out. They don't have complicated ideas about who can sleep on the sofa and the other on the couch. It is a fact that either of them can sleep anywhere they please. Even on the table, should they so desire. But since the lady of the house is looking at the ants, they will too. She has counted each and every one of those ants. She knows where they're going and the crumbs that are going with them.

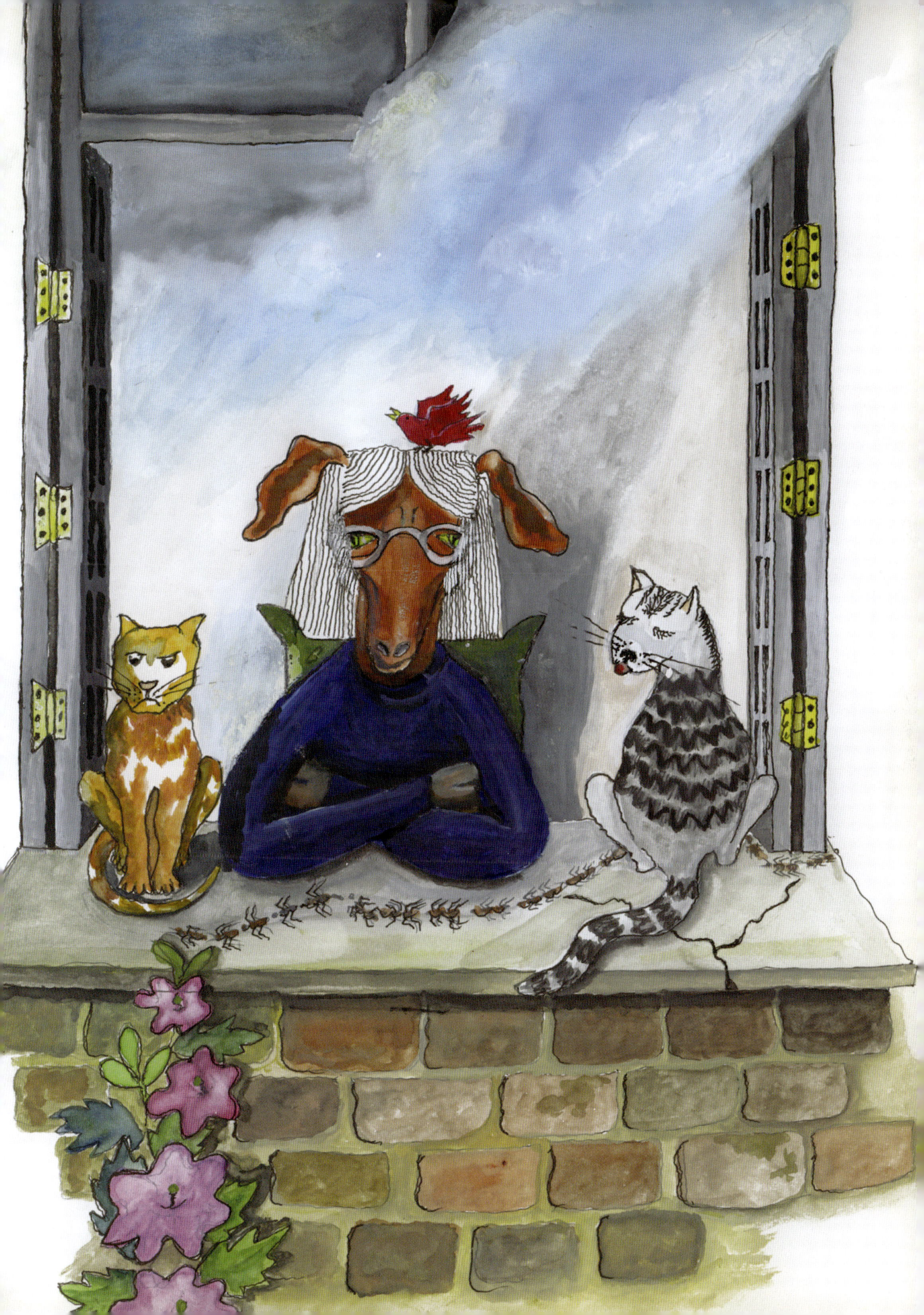

## Kika

The birds that nest in her courtyard are a part of the family. They are welcome in too. Maybe not with the cats. Who decides whether it's the cats or the sparrows? The six chipmunks that reside in the courtyard are fast and furious. No time to squeak to the lady of the house. And the rabbit with its broken leg is hidden under a bush where no dog can find him—because there are dogs in the region, but this sacred corner is forbidden to them. The cows in the pasture across the street remind them that farmers inhabit this planet too. And then the weeds! This one belongs to the crickets. And the ladybugs . . . they have their weeds too. Then the frogs that live on the banks of the canal. And the toads that make that beautiful trilling at night, during the hot season. It's a splendid Earth, if we'd only leave it alone. And that's where my friend Kika lives, on that corner of planet Earth, keeping it as sane as it once was for her and for the critters that live there with her.

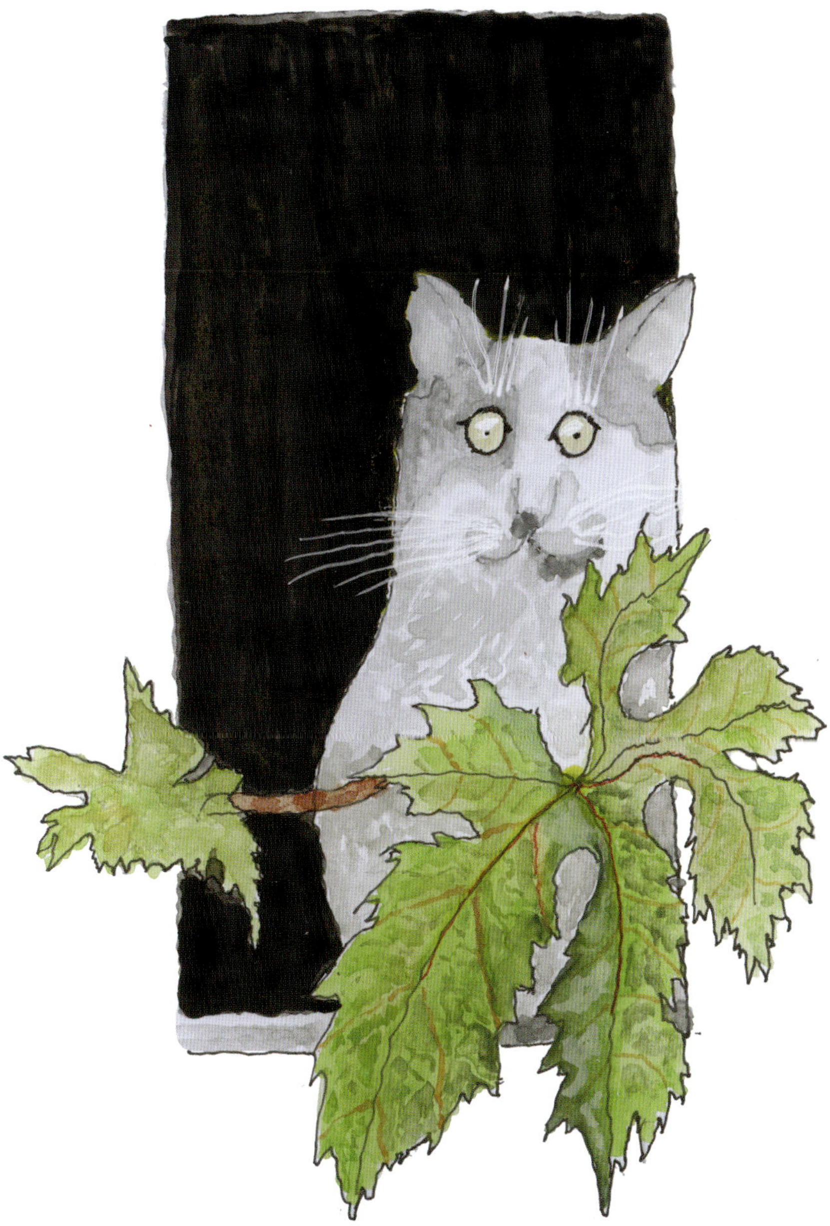

# Tsai

I sent the portrait I had done of him to Tsai, hoping he would like it. He is full of imagination and humor, so I was confident. I soon received a letter from his wife, Pui Di. She told me that Tsai used to play with crickets in the sand dunes and train them to walk. "Your portrait reminded him of his youth."

Tsai added a P.S., saying, "I'll tell you more how one could have a lot of fun . . . not just a Chinese boy but others too, and adults."

I must ask him.

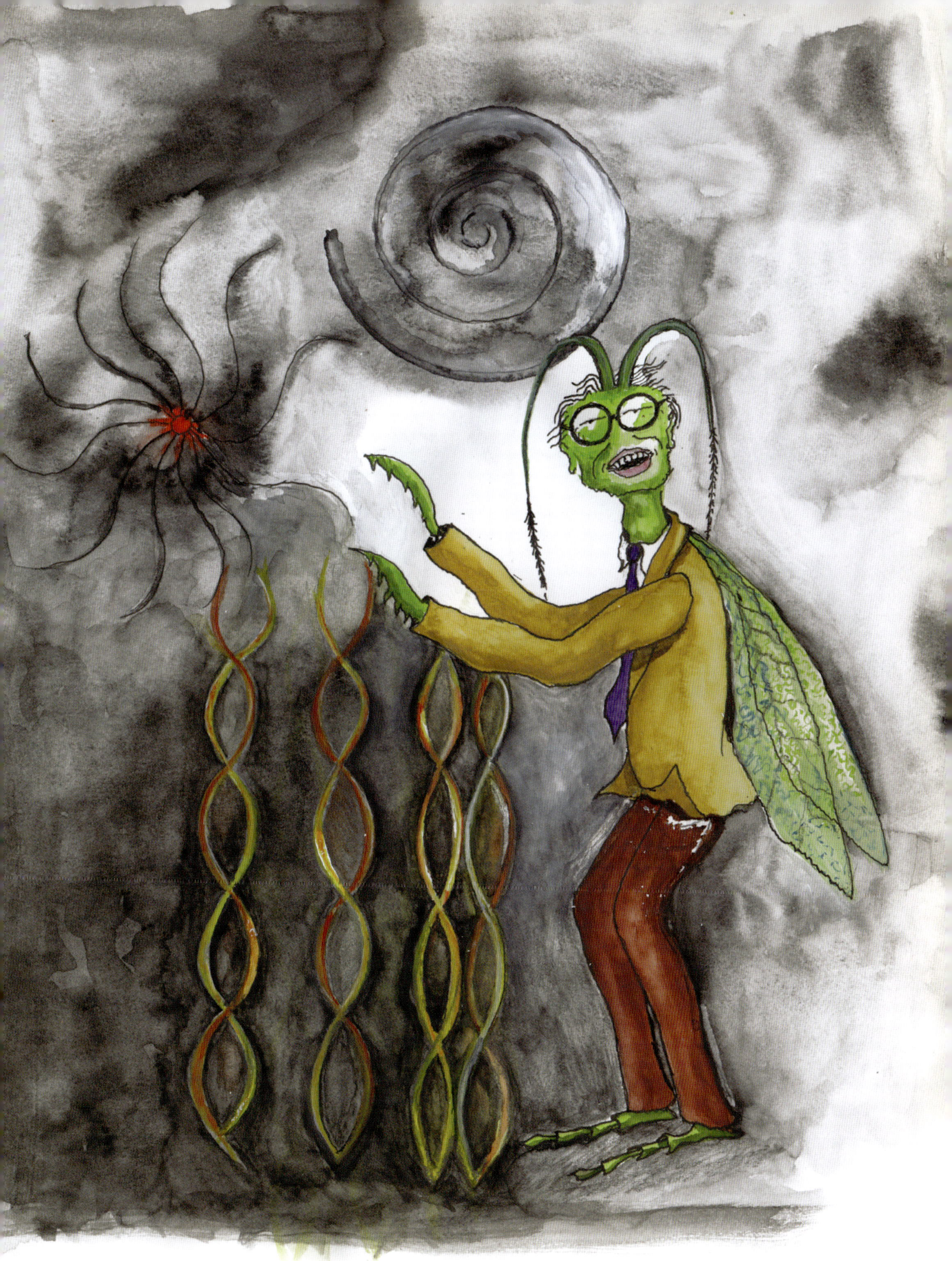

# The Pérous

To play the accordion, you must hold the instrument on your lap, with the strap across your back. Since it's very heavy, it is best held close to your chest to keep it steady. My mother, who was an excellent accordion player, must have played a lot when she was pregnant with me. I have an "all-out tune-in" with the accordion and can hear it miles away. That's why, at a late age, I decided to take lessons.

Please meet my accordion teacher, Gérard Pérou, and his wife, Agnès. They are bicycling around the world. They are learning new music, meeting new people, tasting new food, learning new customs. They have been through South America, the Middle East, and parts of Asia with these heavy suitcases and accordion cases and boots and cameras stacked carefully on their luggage racks. Their last stop was here in New York, where, in my living room, Gérard got out his accordion to play for me! It had been two years since they left home.

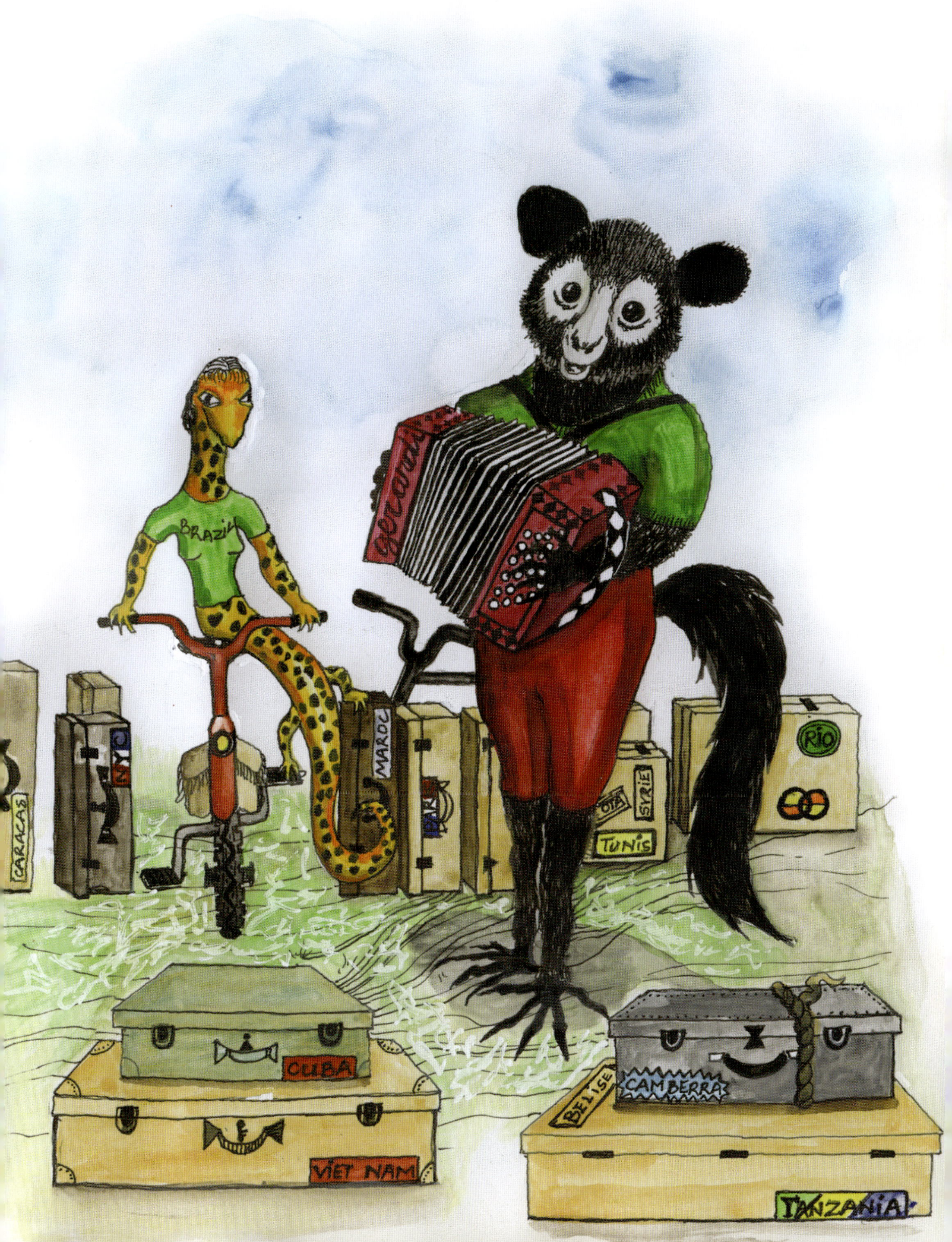
CARACAS
NYC
MAROC
SYRIE
TUNIS
Rio
CUBA
VIET NAM
BELISE
CAMBERRA
TANZANIA

# Aunt Mary by the Sea

My mother was the youngest of three girls born to Louisa and Holton James. Aunt Mary was the middle one, a silver fox. For as long as I knew her, she lived by the sea. Aunt Mary had become deaf at the age of eight, if I remember correctly. She was hit in the head by a swing and wore a hearing aid all her life. She was a loving and caring person. I adored Aunt Mary, as did her second husband, Slater Brown, and many other people too. She was cozy, thoughtful, and enjoyed others. She was one of the first ecologically aware people. After washing her hands, she would dry them with a paper towel and then hang the paper towel up to dry to be used again. This was forty years ago! No one had to tell her about waste. When I went to Concord to visit Grandma James, Aunt Mary was usually there. We would walk around town, asking mothers if I could push their baby carriage. Every single mother knew instinctively that she could trust Aunt Mary, and therefore she could trust me. Nowadays, I'm a grandmother, and mothers look at me as I pass them on the street to make sure I actually do go by!

Aunt Mary was a painter and a good one at that, doing mostly portraits. One of her favorite subjects was her dog Chum, a little mutt who had one eye that looked off to one side and the other that looked at you with hope. He loved her as much as everyone else loved her. She was a silver fox who lived by the sea. A very special person.

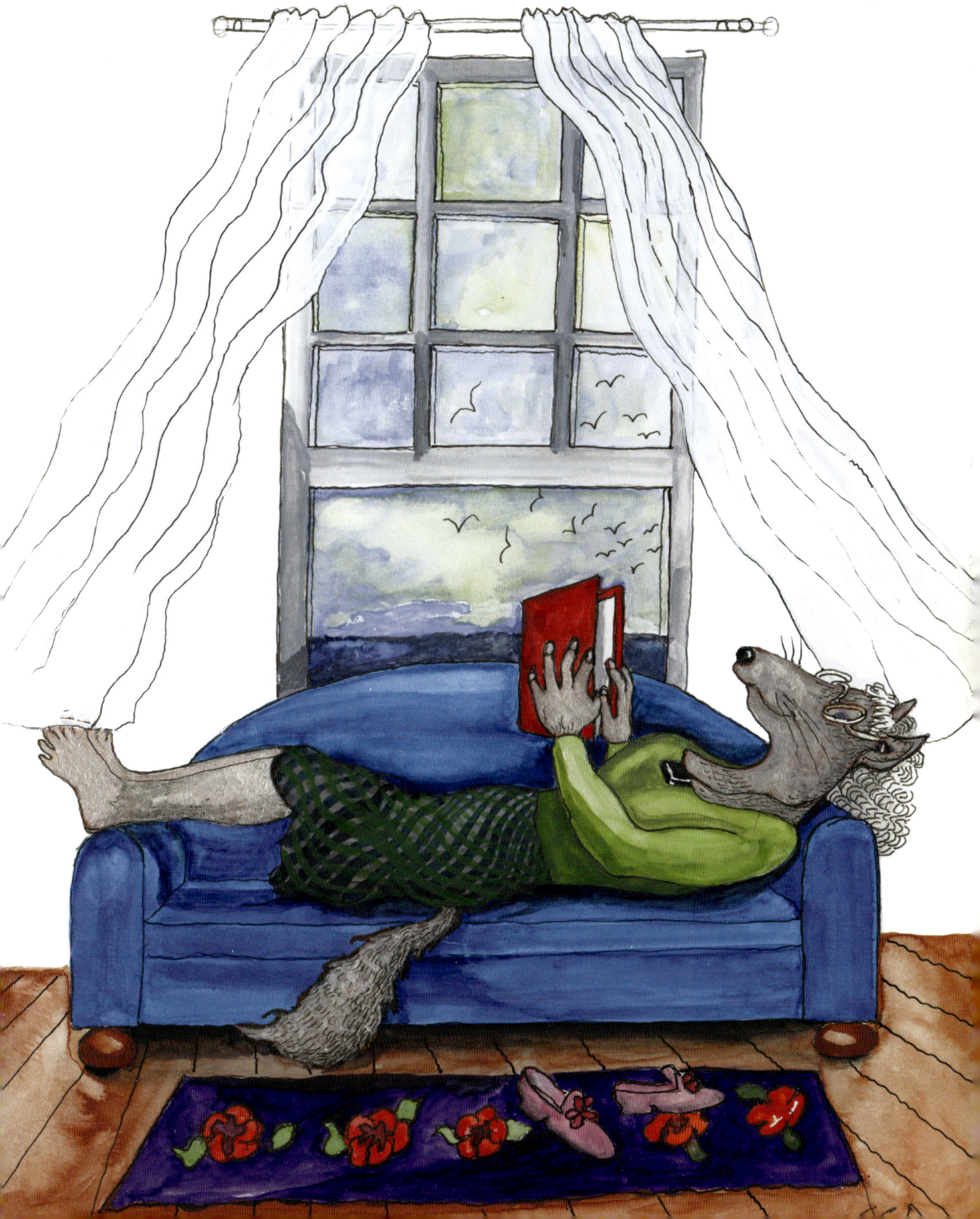

# Oona

Oona, my goddaughter. She dances and she dances and she dances, wiggles, and shakes and swirls and circles and swims and dives and dances across the country and through the towns. What a brilliant idea, and how smart to follow your passion. Following one's passion is what so few people do. You must know how to find your passion. You fumble, you set aside, and you take back. It can be deep down or on the surface. You must find your passion, bring it out, shine it up, keep it well fed, nurture it, and make it yours. Bravo, Oona!

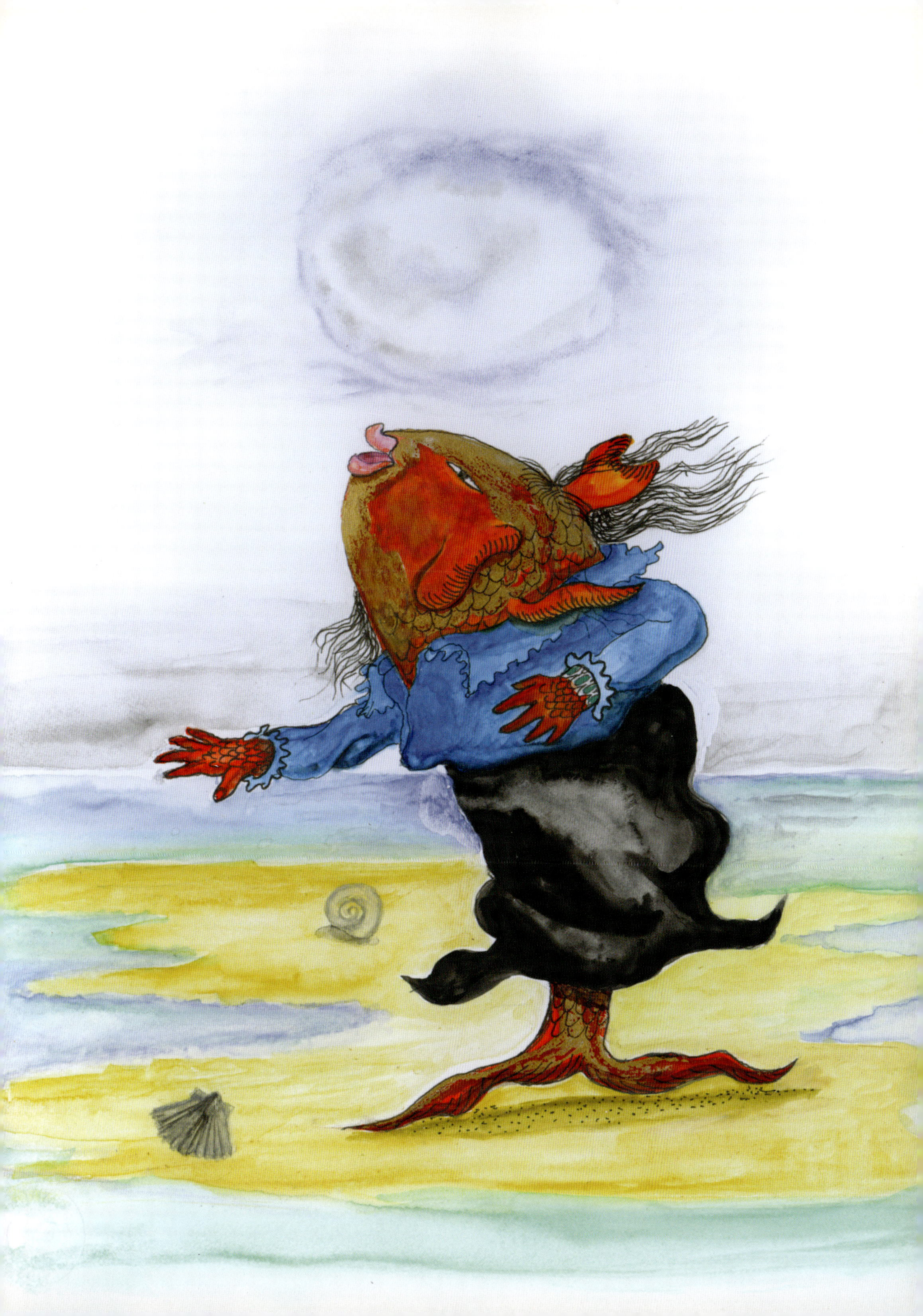

# The Cardinals

I met these compatriots of a different nature in a hotel elevator. They are proud, proud to be true Cardinal fans.

Proud to be Cardinals.

Proud to be two.

Proud to be true fans and proud to be Americans.

Proud to be true!

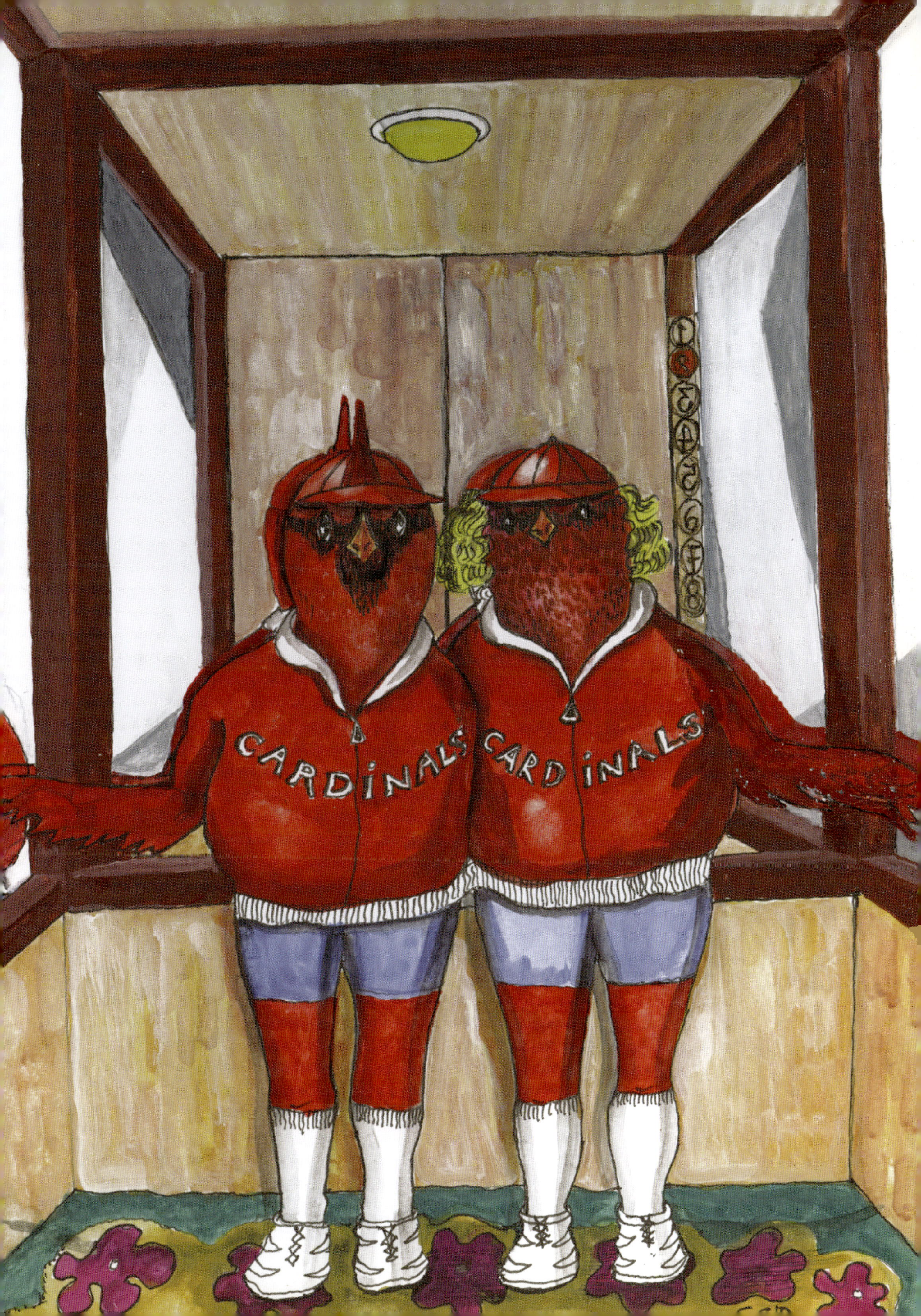
CARDINALS
CARDINALS

# Ingebourg

Ingebourg, the most elegant woman in New York. Even at home when she was serving soup. It just so happens that the soup was delicious too! She and her man lived on Washington Square, so I would say that the only problem was getting up those torturous stone steps that indicate the elegance of the address. She always stood erect . . . not hunched over, even after a day's work at the easel. For she was a painter. I didn't really know her that well, but I imagine that her work clothes were as elegant as her evening clothes. She had Japanese designers worry about her wardrobe. Maybe I should put my mind to finding a Japanese seamstress who could worry about mine. For, to me, it is absolute torture finding something to wear. I don't shop—I don't like clothes shopping—so that makes it all the more difficult. I hate undressing, then dressing into something that may or may not be the winner, then undressing again if it isn't. So, frankly, I do believe that a dressmaker is the only answer for me.

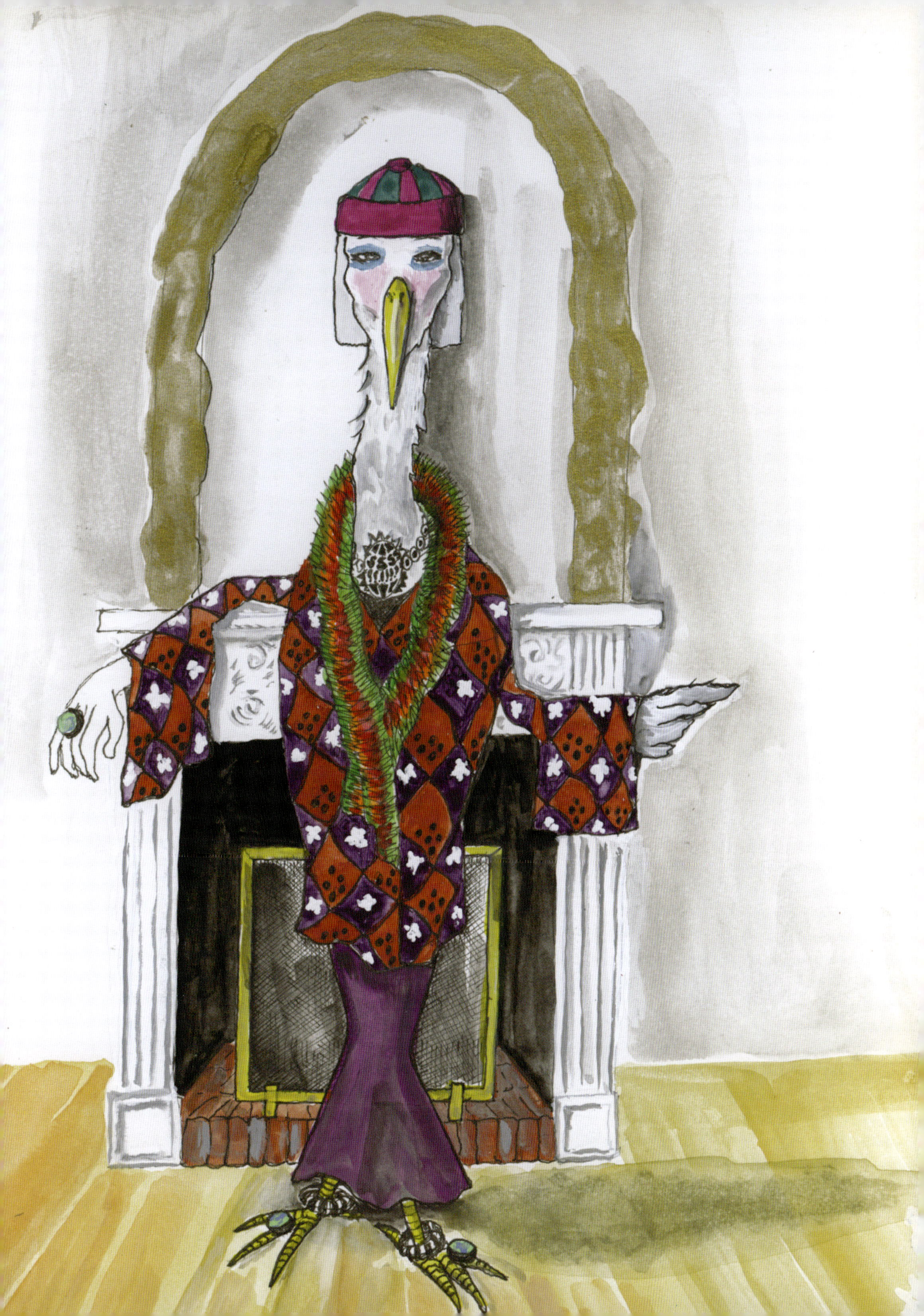

# Chauncey

Chauncey is from Upstate New York. He lives on a huge estate and breeds horses. But if the horses are able to withstand the blizzardy winter, Chauncey is not. So he bought himself a beautiful house overlooking the beach and the Gulf of Mexico on the island of B.G. Chauncey is not often seen by the locals. He doesn't usually attend their daily cocktail parties even when he's invited. He's too rich for them to understand, and it makes him uneasy. He is well-educated: Harvard and Yale. He is on a different island than the locals, though an island with the same name, and he speaks a different language. When his friends from the Northeast come down for a visit to get some sun and rest, he'll invite the locals for a once-a-winter cocktail party. He does have to keep abreast of the island news—after all, the island is an island and a small one at that, and his property depends on the vigilance of the locals. Then at breakfast the next morning, he and his Northeastern friends will entertain themselves by repeating the words of others, the words pronounced by the locals.

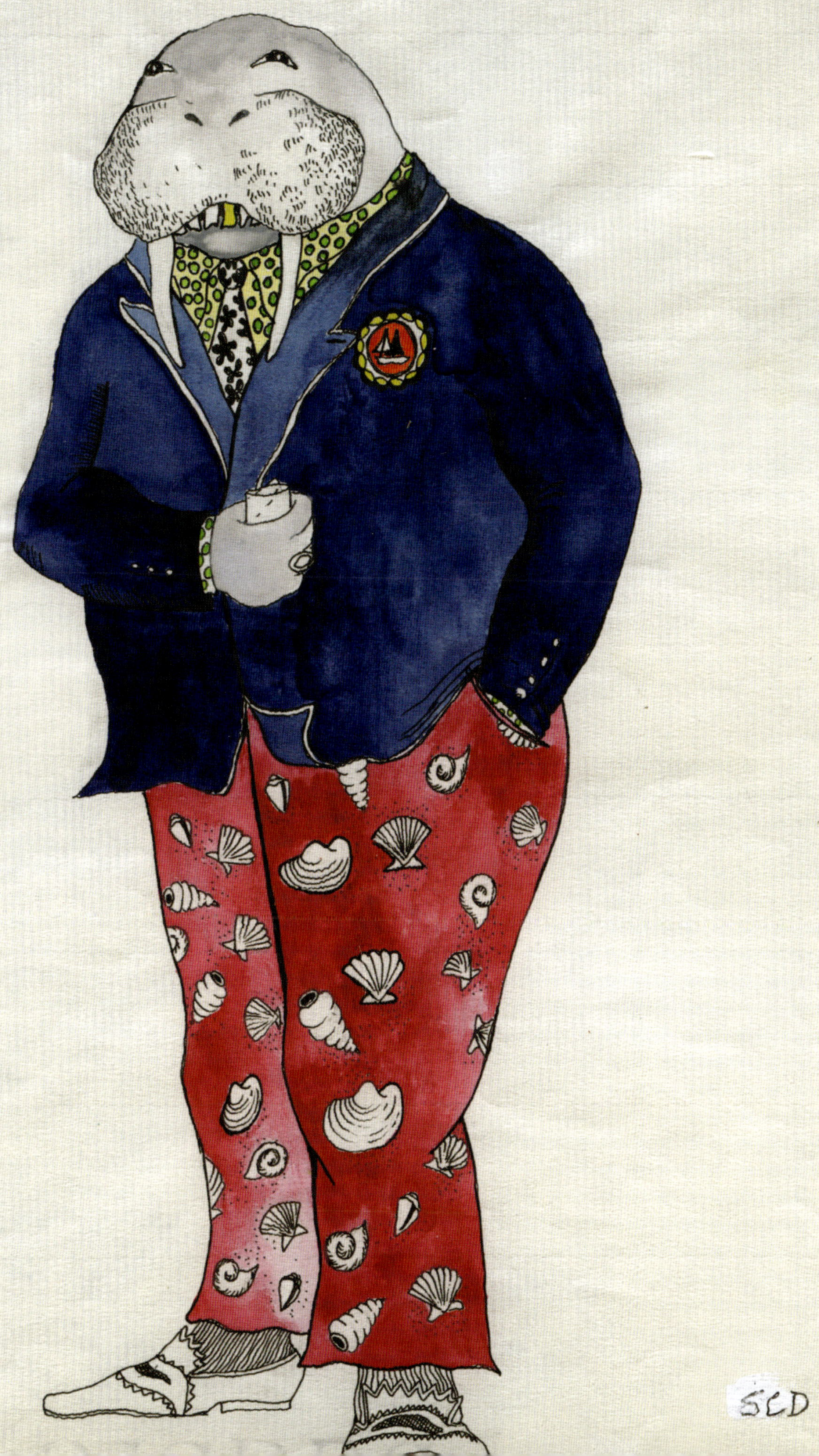
SCD

# Mabeline

Mabeline is from the north side of Chicago. You can imagine the gusts up in Chicago. They get it from the west and from the east: snowstorms, blizzards, williwaws. Everything you can imagine. She says, "It's hard to understand how the Canadians live even farther up north." So, around September-October she gets into her Buick with her cocktail clothes and her summer apparel and says goodbye to her husband, "until later."

She makes her way down along the Mississippi River. When she has made it halfway, she turns left and hits the road toward Florida. She makes it to the island of B.G. in good time. She arrives just in time to do some shopping at Fugates by the railway. She loves hearing the train go through town. It gives her an outer-earth feeling. She will make it just in time for Shirley's, just in time to tell the other snowbirds, as they are called, about her trip down. They will talk and talk and talk. She likes a gin and tonic on ice; she'll slither over and talk with Chauncey. He's the host, and the most respected and the richest millionaire on the island. They have a very courteous and respectful conversation of a few words. Each just wants to reassure the other that nothing has changed on the island . . . and that their serenity is sound and sure. Then, after a last gin and tonic, she'll wander home and throw herself into bed.

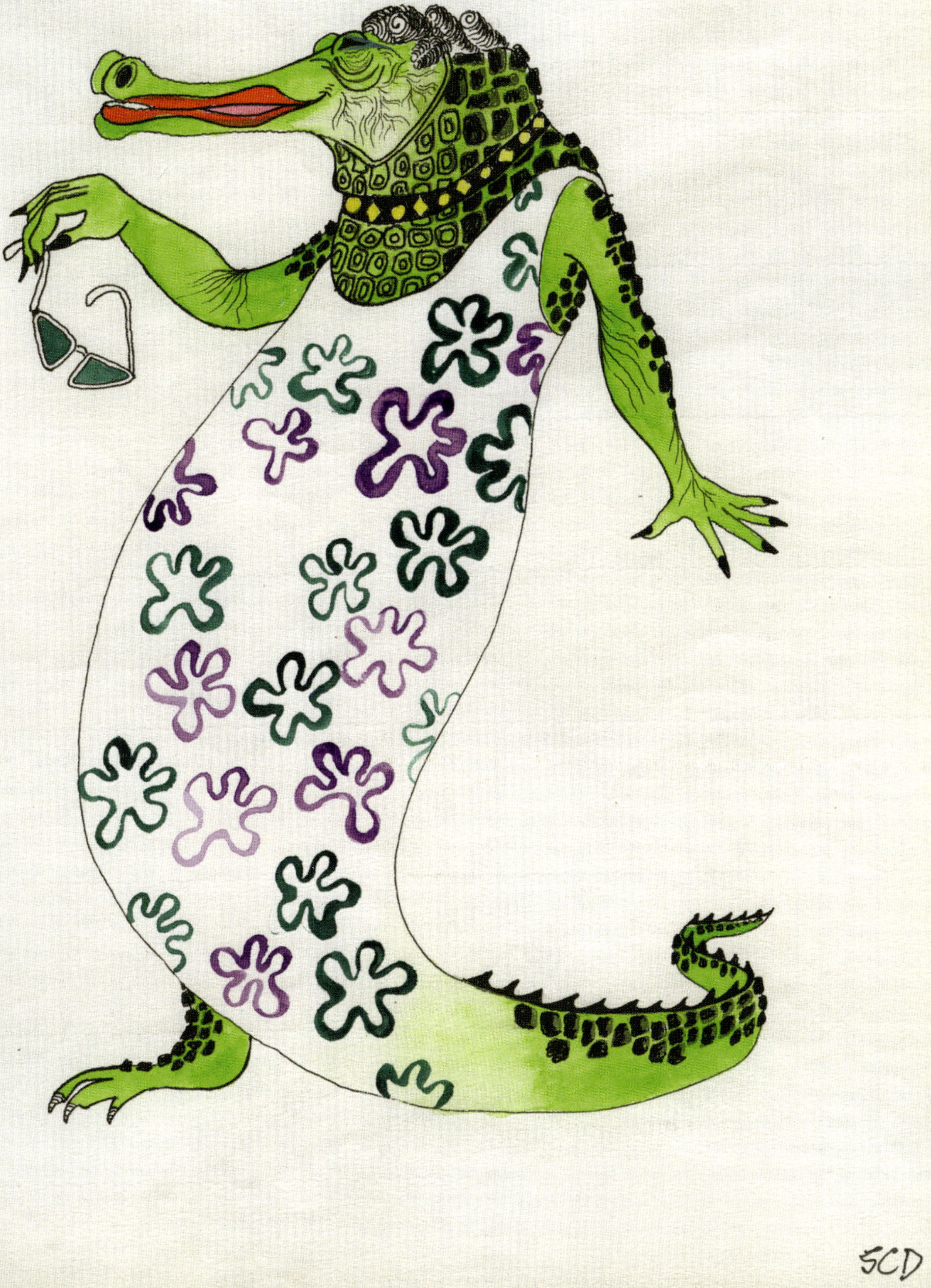
SCD

# A Floridian

Shirley Nable comes from chilly North Dakota. Her husband is a banker. They have enough income to have a winter residence on the warm west coast of Florida. The drifting snow and the howling north winds have sent her south. Who could blame her?

There she can be free and easy and loll around in her flowered pantsuit. She will be with others of her own nature in different pantsuits. One can see in the evening with the orange sunset in the background where the cocktail party is being held. They have parked their cars under the palms trees in front of one house. One can hear the cocktail talk and the laughter floating in the hot air a mile away.

They don't have far to go, so a drink too many is expected. Then tomorrow night they will meet again at Liz Shelby's house. They will meet the same people to say the same things in different pantsuits. On and on, until the end of winter, when they pack up and hit the road once again.

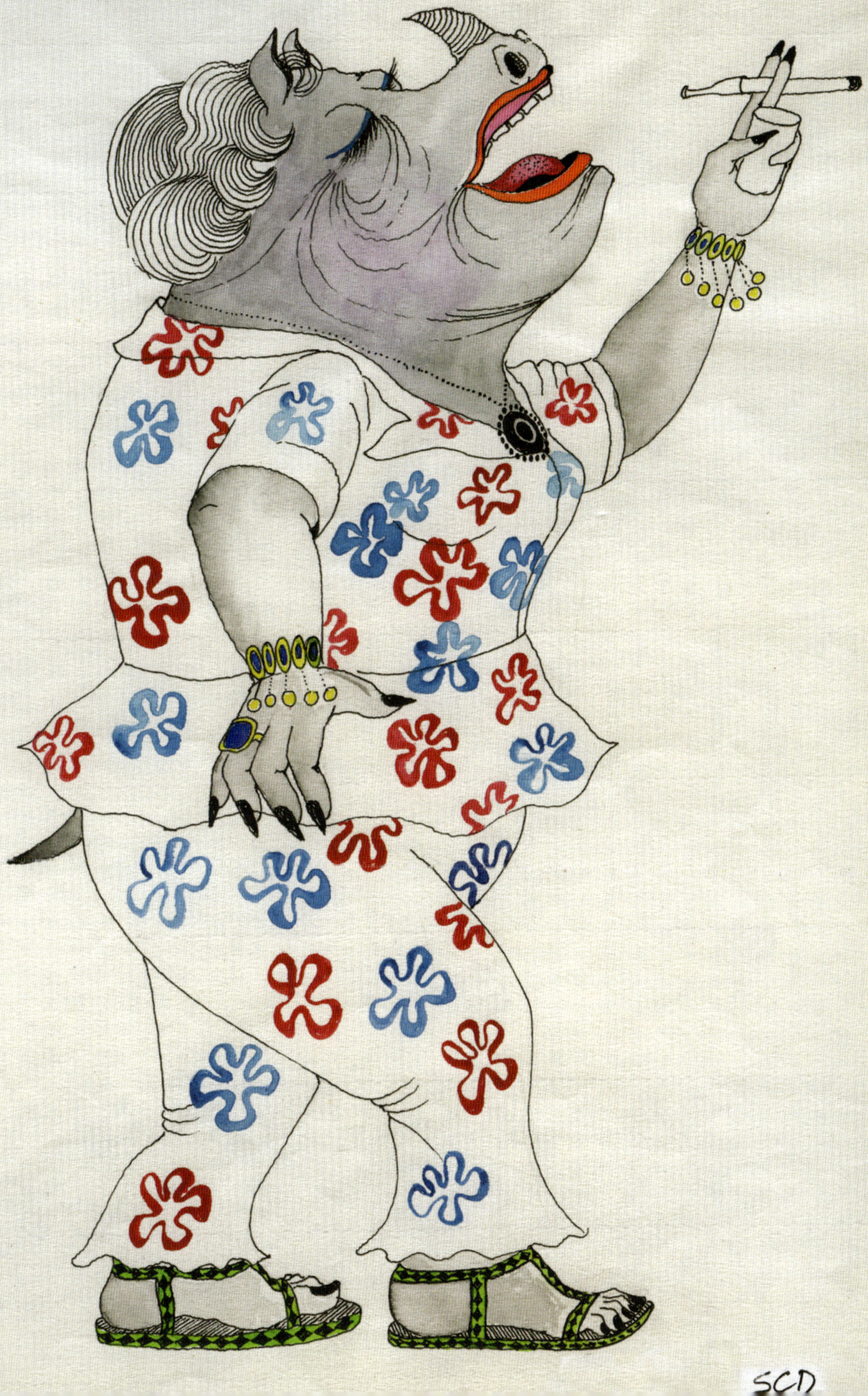
SCD

# Rodriguez

When I first heard him
Singing about the things one sees daily
The hunger, the hypocrisy, the greed and the grime
All that most folks try to dismiss . . .

He points it out in song and rhythm
Striking, then stroking the strings of his guitar
with almighty feeling.

And it hit me right in the face
That this good soul, forty years hence
Still condemns the unfortunate truth
The mighty sad truth,
That never changes.
The ignorance
The suffering
And the crime.

It hurts, it gnaws, it throbs
But it never changes.

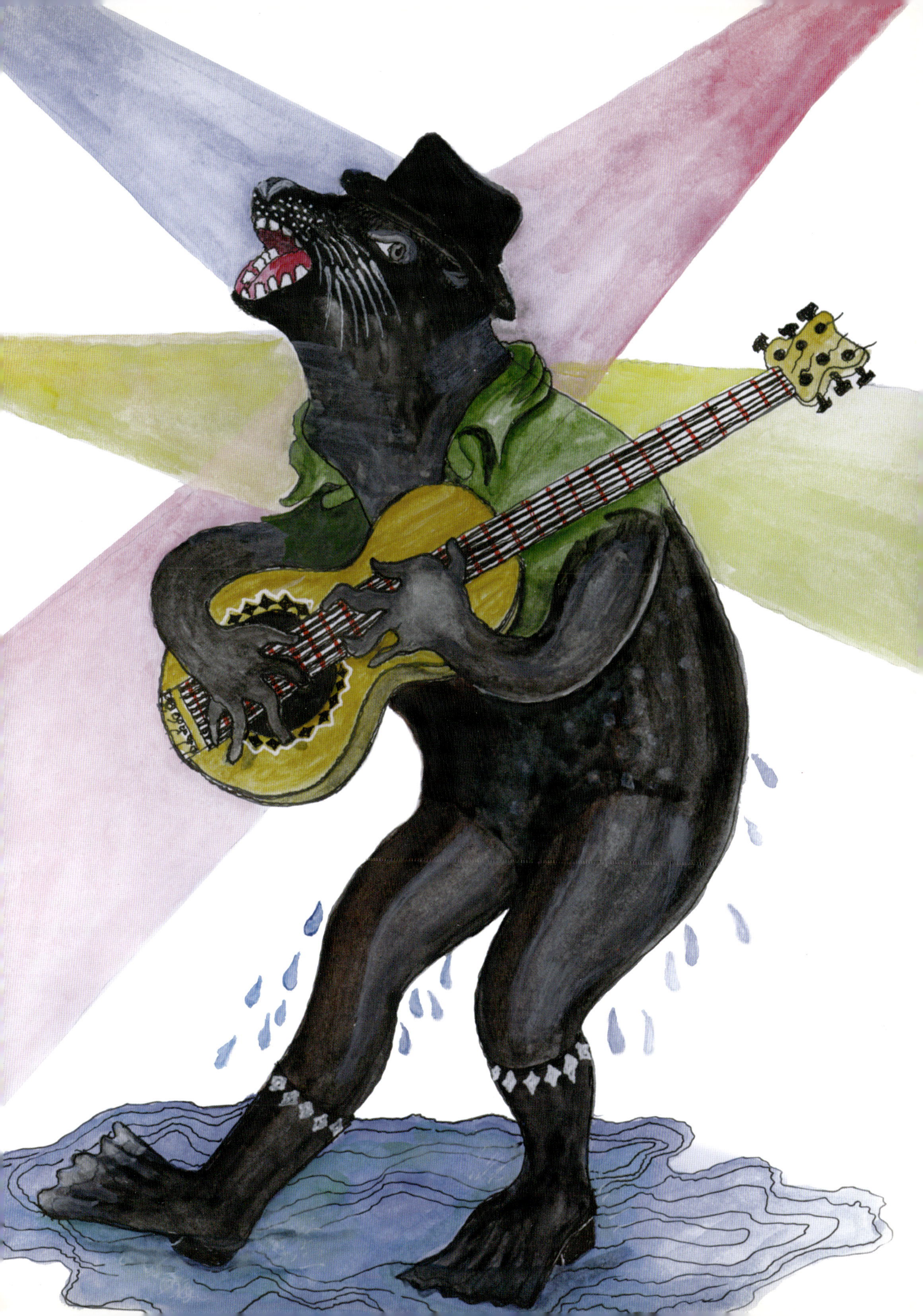

# Flash Friends

Making friends is like entering a cave. It's dark and sometimes damp. You try to unlock the door with the key you were given after shaking hands—"How do you do?"—with, very likely, a flash friend.

Eventually, it could just be a wrong key. There are so many to the front doors of caves. When at last you do find the right one, you carefully turn it in the lock and enter slowly. Hold your arms out in front of you. One never, never knows what lies on the floor, so it's best to keep your arms in front of you in case you trip. A candle is of no use—it would only flicker. Enter slowly. Don't mess around. Examine everything with interest but with a gentle eye. A cave is where you store perishable foods. You might come upon things of special interest, such as a sack of potatoes or a stack of vintage wine.

We met at an opening in France. He and his wife seemed friendly and open. We later met on occasion when I was in France. We phoned each other from our two far-away homes.

"How are you? How is the weather? Ile de Ré? Tivoli? Thank you for the puzzle! And thank you for the warm wishes!"

The phone rang one sunny day.

"We have decided never to see you again!" squawked the belligerent gull, throwing the keys to our friendship into the ocean. I heard them splash into the water and in my ear too.

Rodriquez claims that flash friendships last the time of a hot or cold shower.

What could I have done?

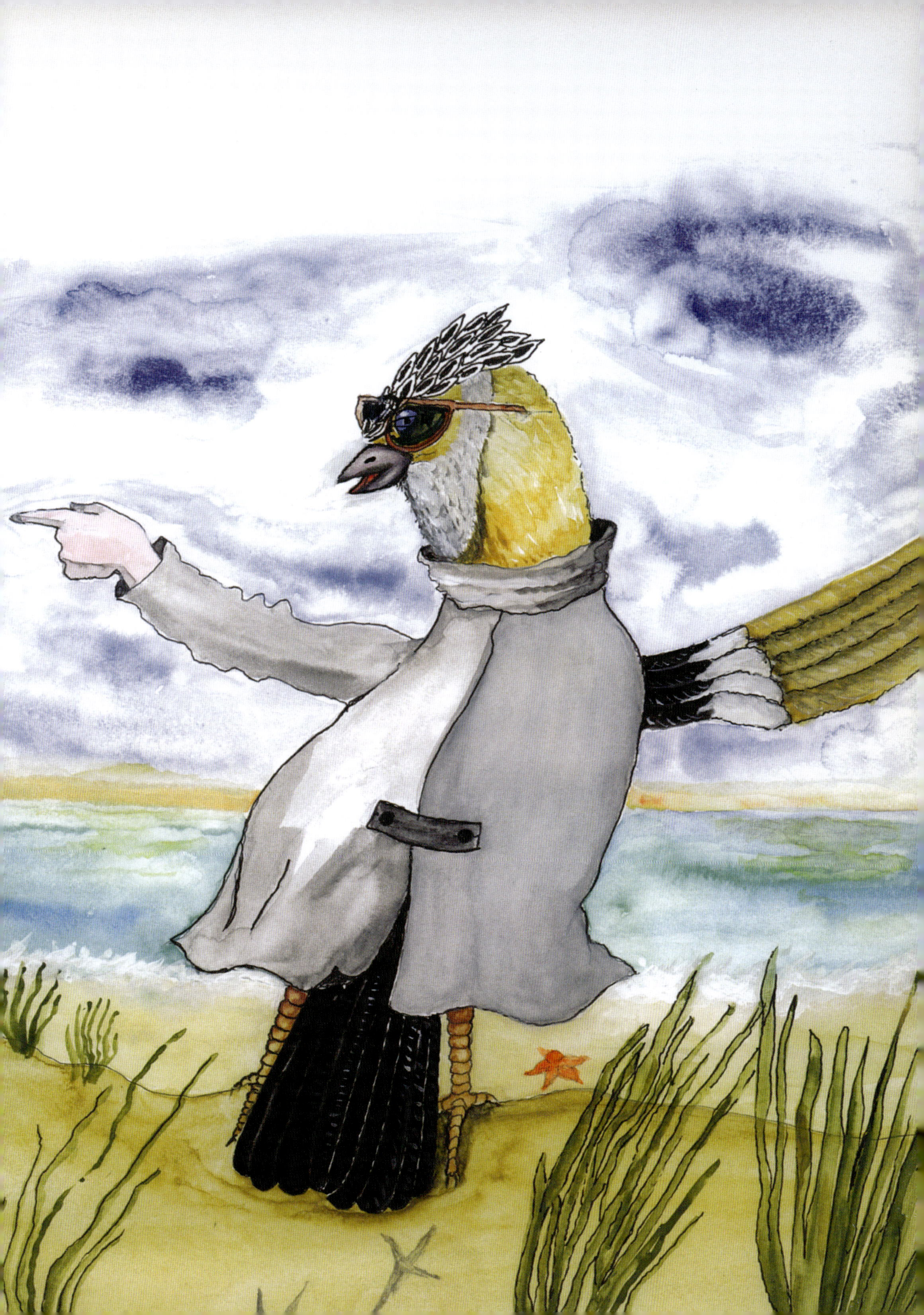

# Last Word

My camel neck has shortened somewhat, and I carry my nose a bit lower. It is a matter of age. Age also helps me tell certain truths.

Listen, it is no secret to me, though maybe it is to you. It is because I am a Calder that this book sits on the table in front of you. Were I a Thimble or a Twitch or a Nimble, it would still be sitting in my closet.

I am very glad to be a Calder, in spite of all the lumps and bumps I might have felt during the trip. And I wish that your trip, no matter what your name may be and in spite of all the jolts and thumps you may have felt, is as enlightening and delightful.

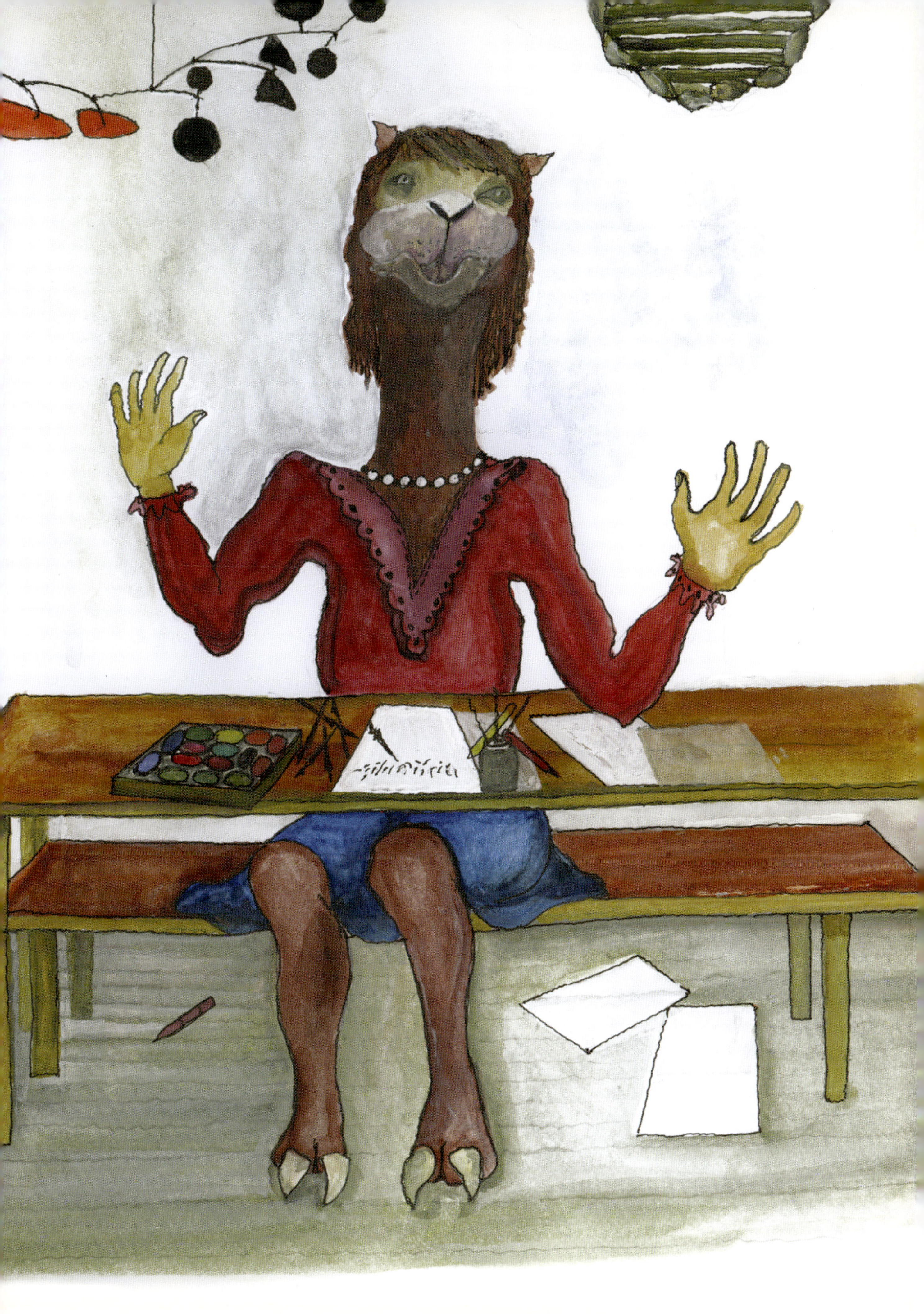

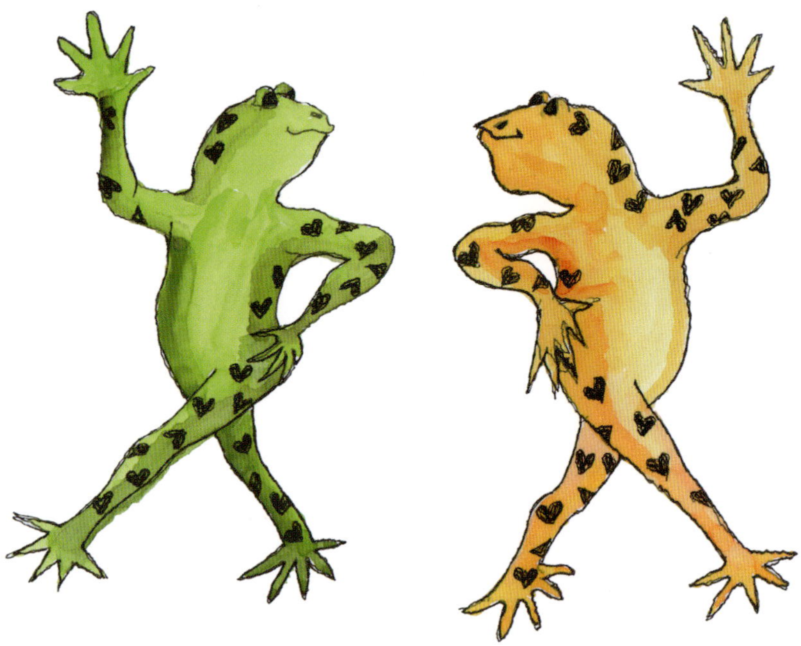